Activating Aesthetics

Activating Aesthetics addresses questions of aesthetics in various fields of education, with the aim of investigating a way of revealing how aesthetics may activate an engaged, responsive and poetic pedagogy. The writers in this collection enliven different ways of thinking about aesthetics, educating through aesthetics and questioning aesthetics. They approach aesthetics through the lenses of art practice and art history, painting and literature, film and popular culture, the built environment and pedagogy, music making and reception, and feminist subjectivity and philosophy. Beyond instrumentalism, each chapter approaches questions of aesthetics by dismantling subject–object separations of analytical aesthetics and opening the potential of aesthetics to work as an activating force in education.

The premise is that education, driven by means–end instrumentalism, may be activated another way via aesthetic encounters premised in difference. To build this argument, the authors engage works of Adorno, Benjamin, Bourdieu, Deleuze, Guattari, Heidegger, Hölderlin, Hokusai, Irigaray, Nietzsche, Sterne and Stiegler. The juxtaposition of these diverse theorists, philosophers, artists and writers makes for a rich tapestry of different perspectives on processes of learning, knowing and being. Aesthetics in activation discloses new ways of thinking about poetic and engaged pedagogy. Through these different perspectives, the whole collection works towards an educational philosophy of aesthetics.

The chapters in this book were originally published as articles in the *Educational Philosophy and Theory* journal.

Elizabeth M. Grierson is Professor at RMIT University, Melbourne, Australia. An Australian lawyer, and a barrister in New Zealand (as Gresson), with a Ph.D. in Education and a Juris Doctor Distinction, she publishes in philosophy of education, aesthetics, law and justice.

T0347522

Educational Philosophy and Theory

Edited by
Peter Roberts, *University of Canterbury, New Zealand*

This series is devoted to cutting-edge scholarship in educational philosophy and theory. Each book in the series focuses on a key theme or thinker and includes essays from a range of contributors. To be published in the series, a book will normally have first appeared as a special issue of *Educational Philosophy and Theory*, one of the premier philosophy of education journals in the world. This provides an assurance for readers of the quality of the work and enhances the visibility of the book in the international philosophy of education community. Books in this series combine creativity with rigour and insight. The series is intended to demonstrate the value of diverse theoretical perspectives in educational discourse, and contributors are invited to draw on literature, art and film as well as traditional philosophical sources in their work. Questions of educational policy and practice will also be addressed. The books published in this series will provide key reference points for subsequent theoretical work by other scholars, and will play a significant role in advancing philosophy of education as a field of study.

Titles in the series include the following:

Activating Aesthetics

Edited by
Elizabeth M. Grierson

Routledge
Taylor & Francis Group

LONDON AND NEW YORK

First published 2018 by Routledge

2 Park Square, Milton Park, Abingdon, Oxfordshire OX14 4RN
52 Vanderbilt Avenue, New York, NY 10017

Routledge is an imprint of the Taylor & Francis Group, an informa business

First issued in paperback 2019

British Library Cataloguing in Publication Data
A catalogue record for this book is available from the British Library

ISBN 13: 978-1-138-09622-6 (hbk)
ISBN 13: 978-0-367-26483-3 (pbk)

Typeset in Plantin
by diacriTech, Chennai

Publisher's Note
The publisher accepts responsibility for any inconsistencies that may have arisen
during the conversion of this book from journal articles to book chapters, namely
the possible inclusion of journal terminology.

Disclaimer
Every effort has been made to contact copyright holders for their permission to
reprint material in this book. The publishers would be grateful to hear from any
copyright holder who is not here acknowledged and will undertake to rectify any
errors or omissions in future editions of this book.

Contents

CONTENTS

Citation Information

The chapters in this book were originally published in the *Educational Philosophy and Theory* journal. When citing this material, please use the original page numbering for each article, as follows:

Chapter 1
Activating Aesthetics: Working with Heidegger and Bourdieu for engaged pedagogy
Elizabeth Grierson
Educational Philosophy and Theory, volume 47, issue 6 (June 2015) pp. 546–562

Chapter 2
Rendering Visible: Painting and sexuate subjectivity
Linda Daley
Educational Philosophy and Theory, volume 47, issue 6 (June 2015) pp. 608–621

Chapter 3
All Things Out of Rule
Nuala Gregory
Educational Philosophy and Theory, volume 47, issue 6 (June 2015) pp. 563–578

Chapter 4
Activating Built Pedagogy: A genealogical exploration of educational space at the University of Auckland Epsom Campus and Business School
Kirsten Locke
Educational Philosophy and Theory, volume 47, issue 6 (June 2015) pp. 596–607

Chapter 5
Artwork as Technics
Mark Jackson
Educational Philosophy and Theory, volume 48, issue 13 (December 2016) pp. 1310–1320

Chapter 6
Katsushika Hokusai and a Poetics of Nostalgia
David Bell
Educational Philosophy and Theory, volume 47, issue 6 (June 2015) pp. 579–595

Chapter 7
Thoughts on Film: Critically engaging with both Adorno and Benjamin
Laura D'Olimpio
Educational Philosophy and Theory, volume 47, issue 6 (June 2015) pp. 622–637

Chapter 8
'Working With' Music: A Heideggerian perspective of music education
David Lines
Educational Philosophy and Theory, volume 37, issue 1 (January 2005) pp. 65–75

For any permission-related enquiries please visit: http://www.tandfonline.com/page/help/permissions

Notes on Contributors

David Bell is Associate Professor in Art Education at the University of Otago, New Zealand. He teaches and researches the visual arts, classics, aesthetics and museums-based education, as well as East-Asian studies, particularly the arts of Japan. His recent publications include *Hokusai's Project: The Articulation of Pictorial Space* (2007) and *Ukiyo-e Explained* (2004), as well as contributions to *The Cambridge Handbook of the Psychology of Aesthetics and the Arts* (2014) and *Chûshingura and Ukiyo-e* (2012).

Linda Daley is a senior lecturer in Literary and Communication Studies at RMIT University, Melbourne, Australia. She holds a Ph.D. in contemporary European thought, and her research focuses on the politics of aesthetic forms and cultural practices. Her current research focuses on the writing of Australian Aboriginal author, Alexis Wright. Her recent publications can be found in the refereed journals *Feminist Theory, Australian Feminist Studies* and *Contemporary Women's Writing*.

Laura D'Olimpio is a senior lecturer in Philosophy at The University of Notre Dame Australia and a regular contributor to The Conversation and Radio National's Philosopher's Zone. She is Chairperson of the Federation of Australasian Philosophy in Schools Associations and co-editor of the *Journal of Philosophy in Schools*. She has published in the areas of philosophical pedagogy, aesthetics and ethics, and her first book, *Media and Moral Education: A Philosophy of Critical Engagement*, is forthcoming as part of the 'Routledge International Studies in the Philosophy of Education' series.

Nuala Gregory is the Deputy Dean of the Faculty of Creative Arts and Industries at the University of Auckland, New Zealand. She is also an artist working in the mediums of painting, printmaking and drawing, and her artwork has been shown in Ireland, the USA, New Zealand, Mexico, China and Japan. A recipient of numerous arts grants and bursaries, she has contributed to the visual arts environment through curation, artistic collaborations, journal articles, international conferences, and the enhancement of visual arts programmes, teaching and infrastructure at tertiary level.

Elizabeth M. Grierson is Professor of Art and Philosophy and an Australian and New Zealand lawyer. After ten years at RMIT University, Australia, she returned to New Zealand to practice as a barrister (as Gresson). She is editor of *ACCESS*, incorporated into the *Educational Philosophy and Theory* journal. She is well published in fields of philosophy of education, art and aesthetics, law and justice, and has held many international positions, including Visiting Research Fellow at the University of Brighton, UK; World Councillor for International Society of Education through Art; Head of School at RMIT University, Australia; and Life Fellow of Royal Society of Arts, UK.

Mark Jackson is Associate Professor of Design at Auckland University of Technology, New Zealand. He received his Ph.D. in Architecture from the University of Sydney in the early 1990s. His research engages the tradition of Continental Philosophy, especially the works of Heidegger, Foucault, Derrida and Agamben. He has published in the fields of architecture, landscape architecture, design cultures, film-philosophy and the visual arts, and has produced a number of film and video works. He is currently developing a monograph publication on aspects of the work of Heidegger, as well as a series of digital films on capital and empire.

David Lines is Associate Professor of Music Education at the University of Auckland, New Zealand. He has worked at all levels of education as both a music and general teacher. His research interests include early childhood arts education, music education philosophy, community music and improvisation. He is editor and co-editor of *Music Education for the New Millennium* (2005) and *Intersecting Cultures in Music and Dance Education: An Oceanic Perspective* (2016). He plays piano in several jazz ensembles and performs regularly in Auckland, New Zealand.

Kirsten Locke is Senior Lecturer at the School of Critical Studies in Education, University of Auckland, New Zealand. As a philosopher of education, she is interested in the history of ideas and their application to education in New Zealand and international contexts. She is particularly interested in the philosophical theories that underpin mass education systems and the importance of arts education to issues of equality and democracy.

Introduction: Situating *Activating Aesthetics*

ELIZABETH M. GRIERSON
Royal Melbourne Institute of Technology (RMIT) University

Thinking about Aesthetics

Activating Aesthetics addresses questions of aesthetics in education. The collection explores aesthetics, the application of aesthetics and the aesthetic sensibility in educational practices and processes. The chapters canvas aesthetic ways of thinking and how such approaches may be understood through philosophies of education.

Broadly speaking, aesthetics, from Greek *aisthesis* perception, is a branch of philosophy that addresses the sensory conditions of perceiving or accessing an object, artwork or artifact, or natural phenomena such as conditions of beauty—with a view to establishing value through aesthetic judgement. In the analytical tradition, there is an assumed separation between the human subject and the object being perceived. It is in the logic of this separation between one entity and another that philosophical questions arise. On the one hand, if the entity as object in the world is available for analysis or judgement, then the logic of metaphysics will be at work. On the other hand, by dismantling the separation of subject and object, then questions of metaphysical logic arise.

The chapters in this collection explore that terrain by engaging with a range of disciplinary positions. Questions seek explanation. How may aesthetic activations arise? What potential is there to disturb normalised conditions of knowledge or being? It will be seen that there are various avenues of thinking about aesthetics, or educating through aesthetics, or questioning aesthetics, as difference starts to mark the aesthetic terrain.

The book illuminates this terrain. The writers approach aesthetics through sites of art practice and art history, painting and literature, film and popular culture, the built environment and pedagogy, music making and its reception, and feminist subjectivity and philosophy. It becomes apparent that each chapter, by its engagement with pedagogical approaches, dismantles subject–object separations as it opens the potential of aesthetics to work as an activating force in education.

Through the writing, there is a lively engagement with works and ideas of diverse theorists, philosophers, artists and writers, including Adorno, Benjamin, Bourdieu, Deleuze, Guattari, Heidegger, Hölderlin, Hokusai, Irigaray, Nietzsche, Sterne and Stiegler. This makes for a rich tapestry of perspectives on processes of learning, knowing and being. The writers approach the illusiveness of aesthetic components in education by intervening in means–end instrumentalism and activating difference. Importunating polemics of the intrinsic worth of aesthetics are for another time.

The Chapters

The book starts with 'Activating Aesthetics: Working with Heidegger and Bourdieu for engaged pedagogy'. Elizabeth Grierson investigates art in urban space via a process of activating the aesthetic potential of public art and design works. The discussion addresses the question of aesthetics in enlightenment and twentieth-century frames by providing a brief synopsis of the ways successive philosophers have considered and theorised aesthetics. Grierson advances how artworks may be approached ontologically, epistemologically and materially through the philosophical lenses of two different thinkers—Heidegger in 'Building Dwelling Thinking' and 'The Origin of the Work of Art', and Bourdieu's work on a theory of practice and habitus. To exemplify the two vastly different philosophical positions, Grierson assigns ontological and epistemological argument to actual works of art and design in urban space. Ultimately, the discussion shows how the activation of aesthetics, in the ways as outlined, may in turn promote an engaged pedagogy.

In 'Rendering Visible: Painting sexuate ontologies', Linda Daley examines Luce Irigaray's aesthetic of sexual difference. Irigaray develops her theories by extrapolating from Paul Klee's idea that the role of painting is to render visible the non-visible rather than represent the visible. This idea is the premise of Irigaray's analyses of phenomenology and psychoanalysis and their respective contributions to understanding art and sexual identity. Daley argues that Irigaray assembles an aesthetic of sexual difference that exceeds the familiar intellectual traditions, one that articulates the encounter of non-visible, material (human and non-human) forces that engender modes of sexuate being and becoming. Extrapolating from Irigaray, the argument further claims that this encounter is the very matter of artistry and art making. Thus, for Daley, as for Irigaray, aesthetics is a matter of going beyond our normative understandings of representing the visible, and towards the invisible forces of sexuate being and becoming. And it is here, beyond patriarchy's normative principles and perspectives, and beyond metaphysical modes of perception, that art making and artistry may open up a site of 'invisible' sensations of being.

In that site of 'artistry', Nuala Gregory works as an artist-researcher. In 'All Things Out of Rule', Gregory activates aesthetics through her artistic practice of drawing and painting, by bringing together the act of mark making in painting and the writings of Laurence Sterne in the eighteenth-century novel, *Tristram Shandy*. It is in the free play of drawn lines, be they textual or graphic, that the notion of 'all things out of rule' finds its situating formation. A typology of lines is woven throughout Sterne's text and reappears, alter-inscribed, in the artworks. Throughout both Sterne's and Gregory's works, a range of lines appears: fractal, nomadic, rectilinear, hylomorphic and the decisively incised line or cut. Each has different effects. To follow these lines is to enter a world of material expressivity, to be exposed to an ontology of becoming and change, and of flows and transformations that overturn the traditional ontology of being and stable identity. Sterne's use of wild digression, doodles and graphisms establishes certain proximity between writing and drawing. Gregory argues that here in the strange event of drawing a line, the passages formulate a differential ontology, an ontology of becoming as exposed by the work of Heidegger, Deleuze and Guattari.

Extending aesthetics to the spatial environment, Kirsten Locke investigates relationships between the built environment and education in 'Activating Built Pedagogy: A genealogical exploration of educational space at the University of Auckland Epsom Campus and Business School'. Locke positions aesthetics in an active relationship with educational policy and practice by considering the nexus of different kinds of architectural environments, disciplinary practices and teaching pedagogy. Her historical discourse of 'vibrant materialities' draws from a Nietzschean genealogical methodology with specific reference to university environments for learning. Locke argues that teaching spaces and the built environment are never neutral; in their activations, they embody the values and purposes of education as an ideological terrain. Aesthetic and social relations are working actively to constitute pedagogies of practice in this genealogical account of different disciplinary practices and values—those of business and education—in a rich and critical perspective on 'built pedagogy'.

In 'Artwork as Technics', Mark Jackson opens discussion on activating aesthetics in educational contexts. He argues that we require some fundamental revision in understanding relations between aesthetics and technology in contexts where education is primarily encountered instrumentally and technologically. Jackson addresses this through the writing of the French theorist of technology, Bernard Stiegler, and extends Stiegler's own discussion on the work of Martin Heidegger concerning the work of art and technology. Crucial to this discussion is recognition of the thinking of the late eighteenth-century German poet, Friedrich Hölderlin, on the work of Heidegger. Jackson questions whether such recognition may extend aspects of Stiegler's own thinking. Through his analyses, Jackson shows relationships between philosophical thinkers on the aesthetics of artworks as technics.

David Bell's 'Katsushika Hokusai and a Poetics of Nostalgia' brings an art historical perspective to the activation of aesthetics. The objects of analysis are the literary and pictorial arts of Japan. By examining the permeation of acute sensitivity to melancholy and time, Bell takes the reader to the medieval courts of Japan and the pervasive 'sense of aware'. Here is a poignant reflection on the pathos of things. This sensibility became the motivating force for court verse, and through this medium, for the mature projects of the ukiyo-e 'floating world picture' of artist Katsushika Hokusai. Hokusai reached back to 'aware sensibilities', subjects and conventions in celebration of the poetic that sustained cultural memories that resonated in classical Japanese lyric and pastoral themes. Bell examines how this elegiac sensibility activated Hokusai's preoccupations with poetic allusion in his late representations of scholar-poets and the unfinished series of Hyakunin isshu uba-ga etoki, 'One hundred poems, by one hundred poets, explained by the nurse'. Bell undertakes a close examination of four artworks to identify the ways aesthetic sensibilities trace through the visual and poetic of historical memory to determine cultural codes and attitudes.

Laura D'Olimpio takes the reader to a consideration of contemporary film in 'Thoughts on Film: Critically engaging with both Adorno and Benjamin'. There is a traditional debate in analytic aesthetics that surrounds the classification of film as 'Art'. While much philosophy on film has moved beyond this debate accepting film as a mass art form, D'Olimpio reconsiders the criticism of film by focusing on the dialogue between Theodor Adorno and Walter Benjamin. Adorno critiques film as 'mass-cult', mass-produced culture that presents a 'flattened' version of reality and encourages passivity in viewers. The dialogue between Adorno and Benjamin is interesting because it raises the possibility of positive emancipatory effects, as well as the negative politicisation effects of film as a storytelling medium, mass-produced and distributed. Reading Adorno alongside Benjamin is a way to highlight the role of the critical thinker as audience. By reconsidering Adorno and Benjamin's theories of mass art, D'Olimpio is championing the activating potential of film for mass culture and the value of critical thinking in the reception of film. Here she argues that the critical thinker is a valuable citizen. The aesthetic of film has a social role, and its ethical values or otherwise may be understood and enlisted by critical reception and dialogue.

The collection concludes with a chapter by David Lines, 'Reconsidering Music's Relational Dimension: Heidegger and the work of music in education'. Lines considers the way and manner in which musicians and music educators approach their work. It is suggested here that anthropomorphic conceptions of music have endured in music education practice in the West. From this contention, Lines proposes that our view of the 'processes' of music making, music reception and music learning may be open to challenge and reconsideration. To assist in this task, Lines draws from Heidegger's theory of art as a way of rethinking these processes and reconsidering our relational dimension with music. The unfolding of music in music events occurs as people 'work with' music and interact with its dimensions in a way that is culturally and dialogically vibrant. Music education can thus become more responsive to changing 'modes of beings' in the moment. Here lies the activating potential of music and the educator's potential to activate music's aesthetic.

Conclusion

In bringing this collection together, it is hoped that the position of aesthetics in philosophy and the philosophy of aesthetics in education may find an authentic focus. Through different perspectives, the collection as a whole works towards an educational philosophy of aesthetics. The writers allow their investigations to speak discursively to aesthetic debates and concerns—and out of this, an understanding of aesthetics for twenty-first-century education becomes fertile ground.

The chapters in this collection have previously appeared as articles in *Educational Philosophy and Theory*; those by Elizabeth Grierson, Linda Daley, Nuala Gregory, Kirsten Locke and David Bell appeared in Vol 47: 6, the first special issue of ACCESS incorporated with EPAT. The issue was called 'Activating Aesthetics'. The chapter by Mark Jackson was published as an article in Vol 48: 13, and the chapter by David Lines in Vol 37: 1. The editor's selection of these writers is well justified as they meet the criteria of addressing aesthetics and working with the philosophies of difference. The aim has been wide but exciting.

At the time of producing the special issue of ACCESS in EPAT 47: 6, esteemed New Zealand professor, Jonathan Ngarimu Mane-Wheoki CNZM died, and the journal issue was dedicated to him. He was a leading scholar of Māori art and ecclesiastical architecture, of Ngāpuhi, Te Aupāuri, Ngōti Kuri and English family descent, and it seems fitting that this book *Activating Aesthetics* also honours him. Professor Mane-Wheoki's approach to teaching and learning encapsulated the value of aesthetics in education.

Activating Aesthetics: Working with Heidegger and Bourdieu for engaged pedagogy

ELIZABETH GRIERSON

Abstract

This article seeks to investigate art in public urban space via a process of activating aesthetics as a way of enhancing pedagogies of engagement. It does this firstly by addressing the question of aesthetics in Enlightenment and twentieth-century frames; then it seeks to understand how artworks may be approached ontologically and epistemologically. The discussion works with the philosophical lenses of two different thinkers: Heidegger, in 'Building Dwelling Thinking' and 'The Origin of the Work of Art', and Marxist sociologist, Bourdieu with his work on a theory of practice and habitus. It asks how art may work in the meaning-making processes of place and the human subject in terms of ontological difference (Heidegger) and dispositional capital (Bourdieu). In bringing these different organising principles of interpretation to specific works of art, the discussion draws from locational research undertaken in Newcastle/Gateshead and Melbourne.

Introduction: Propositions and Positions

This article considers aesthetics and the relations between aesthetics, urban place and the human subject with art as the primary focus. It envisages the potential for a summary of aesthetic theory. It offers a proposition that artworks in public spaces may activate a form of aesthetics that speaks as a form of pedagogy. This activation may open deeper ontological questions regarding historicity of being, which in turn may open to a fundamental ontology of difference. Alongside this ontological position, the discussion posits an epistemological approach to artworks as cultural productions in public space understood via a metaphysical process of presence. This discussion is curious to see how these different approaches may work together, and how the possibility of engaged pedagogy may situate a politics of difference, and thereby an

5

Figure 1: Millennium Bridge over River Tyne, Newcastle/Gateshead
Photographer: Nicholas Gresson 2010

understanding of difference, by virtue of the two vastly different interpretive procedures.

By drawing from Heidegger's texts, 'Building Dwelling Thinking' (Heidegger, 1999a) and 'The Origin of the Work of Art' (Heidegger, 1999b) and Bourdieu's interest in *habitus* through a theory of practice (1977/1972, Bourdieu, 1990/1980), the discussion relays between Heidegger and Bourdieu to see if in fact those two different positions may contribute in discursive fashion to meaning-making processes of place and the human subject. The research is drawn from site visits to Newcastle/Gateshead (Millennium Bridge), Melbourne (McInneny),[1] and Old Melbourne Gaol precinct (Boyce).[2]

Starting Place: The Bridge

> The bridge swings over the stream 'with ease and power.' It does not just connect banks that are already there. The banks emerge as banks only as the bridge crosses the stream. The bridge expressly causes them to lie across from each other. One side is set off against the other by the bridge. ... it brings stream and bank and land into each other's neighbourhood. The bridge gathers the earth as landscape around the stream. ... bridges initiate in many ways. (Heidegger, 1999a, p. 354)

Heidegger is concerned with what things, bridges, buildings, art works 'do' in the world rather than what they 'are' or how they may be appreciated via aesthetic knowledge or an aesthetic attitude. In 'Building Dwelling Thinking' Heidegger asks, 'What is it to dwell? How does building belong to dwelling?' (Heidegger, 1999a, p. 347), addressing these questions by investigating the bridge in terms of its capacity for building and gathering 'as a passage that crosses' (p. 354).

A notion of Heidegger's 'gathering' became clear in the process of walking along the frozen pavements of Tyneside in Newcastle/Gateshead one winter's evening. Behind me was the Tyne Bridge and Robert Stephenson's High Level Bridge, and ahead was a giant arch lighting up the evening sky. Water and sky came together as the iridescent LED saturation of changing colours carved an arc through the gathering darkness. At the time, I did not have foreknowledge of the technological design of the world's first and only 'tilting arc', the Gateshead Millennium Bridge with its 126-m span,[3] the brainchild of Wilkinson Eyre Architects and Gifford engineers. Although captivated by the changing lights against a darkening sky, I was not engaged with the functionality of the cantilevered elliptical arch opening like a 'winking eye' to allow ships up to 25 m above water level to pass beneath. Later, this technological process became clear by witnessing the capabilities of six hydraulic rams powering the electric motors to set in motion the bridge's rotational movement of 40°. Not until it returned to a horizontal equilibrium could foot and cycle traffic cross the River Tyne once more (See Figure 1).

The bridge with its LED lighting was certainly technological, yet there was something more than an overt technological feat here. A gathering was taking place here, in a way that was opening the place to me and me to the place. Of Heidegger, Krell (1999c) had written, 'To the thing as technological component and as scientific object Heidegger opposes the thing as the place where the truth of Being, disclosedness, happens' (p. 344). What, actually, was Heidegger meaning here?

So began the research project of *activating urban aesthetics*: the search to find different ways of interpreting and understanding aesthetics via artworks in urban spaces as a pedagogical procedure. Each research site offered specific artworks through which to trial and extend the investigations of how art may *work* to activate a form of engaged pedagogy. For Heidegger, this activation was necessary to redress a failure in the human and natural sciences to understand and respond to the call of being human in the world. How did Heidegger's *initiating* and *gathering* work in this context?

How Aesthetic Things 'Gather'

> It is proper to every gathering that the gatherers assemble to coordinate their efforts to the sheltering; only when they have gathered together with that end in view do they begin to gather. (Heidegger, Logos, cited in Krell, 1999d, frontispiece)

Heidegger raises a series of questions, leading to a discussion of perceptions of place and ontology; in other words, he was questioning what it might mean to gather or share place as a 'summons into being'. His is an ontological, not epistemological enterprise. He is concerned with 'being in the world' not 'knowing about' the world. This research set out to understand the aesthetic components of artworks in urban spaces, but working with Heidegger soon presented a problem with 'aesthetics' as a way of accessing and analysing objects and artefacts. Then, by working with Bourdieu, aesthetics came into alignment with the politics of power in social structures. Both were dismantling analytical aesthetics, but in different ways.

This discussion focuses on the Gateshead Millennium Bridge, and artworks by McInneny, *Journey's Seed* (McInneny, 2005) and Boyce, *We are Shipwrecked and Landlocked* (Boyce, 2008), to draw Heidegger's philosophical project alongside theories of Bourdieu: an unlikely coupling. Bourdieu's materialist account from a Marxist lineage offers an understanding of what he calls *habitus*, as a site of embodied dispositions conditioned and reproduced by symbolic and institutional systems to produce cultural capital in the realm of practice. Bourdieu occupies a significantly different political position from that of Heidegger as clarified in Bourdieu's writing on Heidegger's political ontology (Bourdieu, 1991). While distanced from Heidegger, Bourdieu also acknowledges a debt to Heidegger by drawing from the philosophical concept of Heidegger's *Dasein*, as 'being-there' in the world, to develop his sociological position of *habitus*. Bourdieu's materialist account of the dispositions of knowledge, his *habitus*, will be addressed further in this paper, in relation to Boyce's work installed at the Old Melbourne Gaol Courtyard. This discussion investigates, through Bourdieu, the capacity of artworks to activate generative relations of production in the webs of cultural practice as situated knowledge. In this, the artwork operates as a field of cultural production, within which and from which a pedagogue may produce and reproduce knowledge of place, time and being. Alongside this approach, through Heidegger there is the project of setting the work of art to work in the world. In this the pedagogue may work with the artwork in its situated surroundings to activate place, time and being as a summons to being.

As the discussion works between Bourdieu's and Heidegger's texts, and applies their texts to specific artworks and locations in the twenty-first century, there is in train an interpretive process in a field of social and philosophical forces different from the cultural and intellectual fields within which the original texts were situated. The times are different, the places are different and the intellectual purposes are different: the differences of these institutional and intellectual mechanisms must be acknowledged as a hermeneutical process. Bourdieu himself wrote of the institutional practices of specific times and the social field that gives rise to the production of philosophical discourses.

Heidegger's account seeks an ontological historicity of art and being. For Heidegger, historicity is understood through time as temporality. Heidegger's temporality is not that of Aristotle's linear time whereby passing moments move from past, into future, through 'now-time' always privileging the linear present. Neither is Heidegger focusing on eternal time as in the 'naturalistic' theism of transcendental thought, nor as in Hegel's thesis on the teleological progression of the human spirit. For Heidegger, time is earthly and anticipatory living towards the finitude of death. In other words, human existence is 'always already' situated in its time of being. An anticipatory *Dasein* throws itself towards its future by seizing hold of the present as 'having-been'.[4] Time is finite. Things in themselves are finite, not appearances or representations of something else in the world. By dismantling dominant Western metaphysical systems of substance, Heidegger situates artworks not as aesthetic objects—made intelligible only through human perceptions of consciousness (as in Hegel), or as social forces of production (as in Bourdieu)—but as events of *disclosure* of the world in us and us in the world. Artworks in their own time enact a kind of revealing process. They reveal a human and community historical sense of what matters to it now: this is an ontological sense, but different from Hegel's systematic ontology of the object and human consciousness with its teleological imposition of history.

By setting aesthetics to work in the world via Heidegger's ontological account, there may be an activation of questions to do with relations between place and being that may act as a form of pedagogical procedure for learning about living at the fundamental level of being human. Alongside this approach, is it possible to identify ways that the practices of art as practices of cultural production in the social world may articulate a *habitus* of dispositions for the human subject to live as a social being? How can a discussion relay across an ontological account and a materialist epistemological account in the one discursive space? Must the project of dismantling aesthetics occur first and foremost in light of Heidegger's enterprise of putting art *to work* as an event of disclosure, and Bourdieu's account of art as symbolic capital? What capacity do artworks have to open the potential for pedagogical possibilities through understanding aesthetics in these differing ways?

Aesthetics: A Brief Exposition

It was during the Enlightenment years that German philosopher, Baumgarten (1714–62),[5] coined the term *aesthetics*, deriving it from Greek *aisthesis* perception. For Baumgarten *aesthetics* existed in the science of *aisthêta* (matters accessed via senses, i.e. non-facts) compared to *noêma* (matters accessed through logical thought process, i.e. facts). The privileging of *aisthêta* did not, however, divorce aesthetics from logical reasoning in the realm of contemplating one's relation to 'the beautiful': there was an emotional aspect to the logical reasoning. Baumgarten saw aesthetics as a kind of science, a rational category of thought pertaining to sensory cognition and art as occupying a place in both sensory and intellectual terms within such cognition.

In the work of Kant (*Critique of Judgement*, 1790), there is a natural purposive or teleological system of knowledge from God, and within this system is the existence of ultimate beauty. The goal of art must be beauty, all judgements of beauty being subjective with an ideal consensus through pleasure, which *ought* to be derived from purposive experience. Dickie (1997, p. 22) sums up Kant's theory of beauty:

> Kant divides the discussion of his theory of beauty into four parts, each of which treats a major concept. … (1) disinterestedness, (2) universality, (3) necessity, and (4) the form of purpose. The theory may be summarized in a sentence: A judgement of beauty is a disinterested, universal, and necessary judgement concerning the pleasure that everyone *ought* to derive from the experience of a form of purpose.

Tracing aesthetics from Kant to Schopenhauer, aesthetics departs from theories of taste as a form of purpose, and enters the realm of 'aesthetic contemplation' as an objective site. Human beings become 'subjects of knowledge' with capacities for aesthetic consciousness as Schopenhauer argued in *The World as Will and Idea* (1883). That Schopenhauer explicitly excluded unpleasant or nauseating objects from the aesthetic consciousness shows that he held to the metaphysical project of substance. The Platonic Ideal of beauty was conceived as a site of contemplation accessible via cognition in a will-less state of contemplation and in the service of the greater (cosmic) Will. In other words, a will-less contemplation of appearances became a site of aesthetic value. For Schopenhauer, attention became somehow distanced and free of the interruptions of our desire, our will freed from our desire.

Hegel proposed a comprehensive aesthetic theory in terms of his progression of the human spirit, whereby 'all dialectical thought-paths lead to the Absolute Idea and to the knowledge of it which is itself' (Findlay, 1977, p. vii). Hegel's universal theory of beauty in the art object belongs to the human spirit coursing through history, as a teleological self-realisation. '[T]he object represented becomes the property of pure self-consciousness ...' (Hegel, 1977/1807, p. 19). As Kant proposed a purposive aesthetic experience, so Hegel's aesthetic theory, which was presented in a series of lectures and compiled by one of Hegel's students, Heinrich Gustav Hotho, positioned the content of art in concert with beauty as the most profound access to what is real for human consciousness—the embodiment of spirit. For Hegel, aesthetics concerns experiencing beauty in art rather than beauty in nature. Through the absolute spirit of art, religion and philosophy, the mind may contemplate the reality of life; the art object manifests 'idea', which holds an essential nature as the embodiment of thought itself. Human form in art holds the capacity for embodying the highest ideal of human nature, mind, reason and spirit. If art has a purpose it is not one of representation of nature or of belief, nor is it one of decoration; rather, it is to provide a source of contemplation of the highest spiritual ideal to which the human mind may aspire and through which the mind may find self-understanding. However, the great classical forms of ancient Greece, which embodied this ideal, have become effete. In this, Hegel utters the end of art, as it was known, the end of absolute spirit in the classical human form, the end of art's defining cultural role.

The twentieth century ushers in processes of engaging, questioning and displacing these aesthetic theories and dispositions. It is important to recognise that such understandings of aesthetics are not transplanted by other theories; rather, the lineages trace and thread through subsequent polemics on art and aesthetics. For example, lineages of Kant's disinterestedness in the 'aesthetic attitude' are evident in theories proposed by Edward Bullough (arguing dispassionate detachment) and Jerome Stolnitz (isolating an object from any hint of a practical attitude). The 'aesthetic attitude' has been much disputed by Dickie (1964), who also entered into debate with Beardsley, disputing Beardsley's theory of 'aesthetic experience',[6] which Beardsley proposed as an alternative to the aesthetic attitude. Seeking to distinguish aesthetic objects from other things, and establishing a series of classificatory criteria and exclusions, Beardsley claimed that the criteria of distinctness, perceptibility and perceptual properties must be met if the end result of aesthetic experience is to be achieved. In *Aesthetics* (1958) Beardsley proposes that focus, intensity and unity (coherence, completeness) must be held in common by all who experience an object aesthetically, and this has nothing to do with artist's intentions, which were excluded from his classificatory criteria. Thus, resolve, equilibrium and order become essential elements in his highly structuralist and instrumentalised account of aesthetic experience.

Heidegger's Project

Just as these polemical theories engaged and questioned their antecedent theories and philosophical positions, so Heidegger both engaged with and displaced a Hegelian position on aesthetics, which had in its turn, engaged the project of German Idealism following Kant. Heidegger would displace the aesthetic attitude and aesthetic experience, focusing on a fundamental critique of phenomena in the world such as the work of art, and more particularly the human subject as a site of presence. For Heidegger, drawing from Husserl, the 'founder' of phenomenology, this meant dismantling the subject from within; in other words, a refusal of metaphysics. This necessitated a rethinking of phenomenology as an instrumentalised process of the human subject experiencing and knowing objects 'out there' in the world. Heidegger questions the deepest levels of knowing as intentional beings. He moves away from appearance (phenomenon) in the Kantian tradition (a thing, such as art, as object of consciousness) and towards understanding the object (or thing) in itself (noumenon) through the ontology of difference. For Heidegger to experience an object as appearance (how it appears to one's conscious mind), per Hegel, is derivative or second hand. He is seeking something other than mere appearance, something that has been concealed by the philosophical project of metaphysics—both in the way consciousness is assumed and in the history of philosophy as a system of *logos*.

Truth, *alētheia*, to Heidegger is 'unconcealment'. Here, Heidegger is engaging with Hegel and the idea of art giving access to the human spirit or truth. In dismantling metaphysics, there is a radical questioning of appearances as sanctioned by humanist thinking, which Heidegger discusses in his 'Letter on Humanism' (Heidegger, 1999c). It logically follows that with the dismantling of appearances in the world, concepts of aesthetic attitude and aesthetic experience cease to exist as something to be intelligibly grasped and analysed via a systematic logic in political and social philosophy. Heidegger (1977) cautions against 'our sheer aesthetic-mindedness' (p. 35), which attitude divorces the need to 'guard and preserve the coming to presence of art' (p. 35).

The above begs the question, where does this leave the art object as a 'thing' in the world, and how does one speak of an experience of art in a way other than through an aesthetic framework? With the dismantling of aesthetic experiences and responses from the evaluative arsenal of art, the positioning of art and one's experience of it becomes forseeable in another way.

Heidegger's project is ontological—he investigates phenomena that exist in the world, including Being (*Dasein*) and the question of Being as existence (which he asks in *Being and Time*, 1927/1962). Heidegger's entire project is the meaning of Being, the ontological question of beings—as art, technology and human beings—and being (living) in the world. In his 1936s lecture, which became the essay 'The Origin of the Work of Art' (Heidegger, 1999b) Heidegger discusses the being of art. But Hegel's position that, 'art is, and remains for us, on the side of its highest destiny, a thing of the past' (Hegel, 1993/1886, p. 13) is challenged by Heidegger. For Heidegger shows how art's potential as a thing in the world is to act as a form of *disclosure* in its time of being. For Heidegger, the concept of time holds a crucial place in his thesis on Being; *as Hegel sees progressive time, Heidegger interrupts time.*

Krell explains how Heidegger shows that 'revelation belongs to every work of art: the work erects a *world*, which in turn opens a space for man and things' (Krell, 1999b, p. 141, emphasis in original). For Heidegger art is a setting forth or becoming of truth, *not truth as an entity*, but as a revelation of the 'world' or 'earth'. Heidegger's 'world' is the everyday horizon of our existence; and 'earth', as 'creative strife', is that which appears in the poems, 'Germania' and 'The Rhine' by German poet, Friedrich Hölderlin, which poems Heidegger lectured on at Freiburg University in 1934–1935. Hölderlin's poetic debt to Homer may be read in *Homer's Hymn* number 30, 'Gaia! Allmother will I sing! Revered/ Firmgrounded nourisher of everything on earth ...' (Homer, cited in Krell, 1999b, p. 142). Heidegger's debt to Hölderlin may be evidenced in the position of earth as affording protection and nourishment: 'In a sense all artwork and all thinking are for [Heidegger] participations in the creative strife of world and earth: they reveal beings and let them come to radiant appearance, but only by cultivating and safeguarding their provenance ...' (Krell, 1999b, p. 142).

Thus, Heidegger is not approaching art in terms of a Kantian universal judgement and purpose: the art object is not a source of contemplation or of disinterested aesthetic judgement. Heidegger dismantles aesthetics in the classical meaning of analytical aesthetics, which eclipses art's ontology, and he puts the inherent capacities of the thing called art *to work* in his ontological project of 'unconcealment'. This 'unconcealment' is 'presencing' in a way that is different from the Aristotlean priority of Being as presence (*Anwesenheit*). Heidegger is not, however, arguing from an anti-Being or anti-aesthetic position; he does not set up one thesis against another thesis to find a synthesis. Rather, working with an ontological difference, Heidegger is dismantling, from within, Western philosophy's ontological position fundamental to the metaphysics of presence. Heidegger's ontology is situated in difference, an ontological difference to be exact. He does not position 'this entity' as different from 'that entity', as an observable and comparative difference of objective entities whose self-contained identities are already present or known. Heidegger's ontological difference is a concept of identity that is constituted *in difference*, in other words in the ever-changing sets of relations in which it finds itself.

Heidegger is not going to brook Hegelian self-actualising processes or progressive consciousness, nor is he working with art to substantiate Kantian judgements of taste. Art is not seeking to achieve 'beauty' as a Platonic Ideal form, nor is it available merely for its emblematic function of identity formation. Heidegger's art is impliedly working in and towards its potential as a temporal and spatial form of *disclosure* of place and being.[7] The concept of disclosure can be brought into alliance with Heidegger's work on the notion of *building* as a form of *dwelling*, which he addresses in his essay, 'Building Dwelling Thinking' (Heidegger, 1999a). As shown above, with the bridge, Heidegger attends to the relation between building and dwelling, and the kind of thinking and being that can arise within this relation: this, the ontological position of difference. Heidegger takes thinking of 'bridge' from 'a mere bridge and then afterward a symbol ... in the sense that it expresses something that strictly speaking does not belong to it' to a bridge that 'gathers to itself in its own way earth and sky, divinities and mortals' (Heidegger, 1999a, p. 355, emphasis in original). The former bridge is 'represented as an unknown X to which perceptible properties are attached' (p. 355). This is what Heidegger is dismantling.

If, as Heidegger posits, there is a relation between building and dwelling, then is it possible for artworks—and bridges—to construct a kind of condition about one's relation to place? Such a question follows another logic, one that is different from that of an aesthetic attitude or experience of art, artefact or bridge, as an appearance in the world or representation of an entity in the world. The question opens to the suggestion that an artwork—as with a bridge—works in its event-ness as a meaning-making strategy in the temporality of Being, opening to the creative strife of earth. For Heidegger this event-ness works as a form of disclosure of the 'being' of the artwork (its ontology), not as an appearance or a representation of some external entity that may be made intelligible by our consciousness; nor to be understood via any aesthetic judgement, attitude or experience. If an artwork is set to work in time and place, then is it possible for this to have any pedagogical affect?

Heidegger calls for openness to the present locale as the temporality of Being. As Charles Guignon (2006) wrote, 'What is needed, then, is a way of recovering a sense of openness of the possible and of our own responsibility as individuals in articulating and bringing to realisation the worldly contexts in which we find ourselves' (p. 30). Pedagogical positions start to become apparent. The artwork is working to disclose the locale in which it is situated, and itself as a locale—'The bridge is a locale' said Heidegger (1999a, p. 357)—and in that locale the human being may be awakened to the 'creative strife' of 'earth'. In this space learning may occur if, and only if, the site of struggle is acknowledged: learning about life, self and earth as the creative struggle for meaning-making as a way of letting truth work through the language, thought and work of art.

Journey's Seed

How does the artwork *work* in the public realm? In 'The Origin of the Work of Art' (1999b), Heidegger's methodology sets the questions of art, work and truth to work through his hermeneutical circles of question and example. 'The Origin of the Work of Art' went through several incarnations, from its birth as a public lecture in Freiburg in 1935, then presented in Zurich in 1936, expanded later that year and presented again in three sections in Freiburg and reworked for publication in 1950 and 1960. Questions on the 'thing' called art grew from the earlier attention to the essence of art in terms of truth and being, with artist and artwork each being a source of the other. In his process of questioning Heidegger asks, 'What does the work, as work, set up?' In its setting, he argues, the artwork is more than its 'object-being' when it 'opens up a *world* and keeps it abidingly in force' (Heidegger, 1999b, p. 169, emphasis in original). For Heidegger, there is another way of learning, another pedagogy beyond the rational scientific mode of making appearances intelligible via cognition or consciousness. How may this be set to work in works of art in public space?

The public artwork of artist, McInneny, *Journey's Seed* (2005)[8] is located at Box Hill in the City of Whitehorse approximately 13 km from the centre of the City of Melbourne, Victoria, Australia. *Journey's Seed* comprises two polished and spun, stainless steel, sculptural forms situated in a space between a tramline and a busy street of this outer transit suburb. The site beside the tram terminus is a space of gathering, moving, crossing paths, stopping, talking, negotiating and navigating daily journeys; it is essentially cosmopolitan, metropolitan. A descriptive account tells of the reflective surfaces lending a floating quality, a lightness and rhythm, to what are in reality solid forms (Figure 2).

Considering the artwork through Heidegger's ontological enterprise, the polished surfaces of the artwork are acting as an event, opening up or disclosing the world of the artwork. There is an activating process at play between the artwork and its surroundings. Each is working to disclose the other, not to explain or to call for explanation. Not only are these activations occurring in the physical space of the sculptures, but also in the informing narratives of the work, in that the artist gathered stories from residents of Whitehorse 'about their journeys and sense of place and space' (Architects for Peace, 2011). Those stories are also contingent on difference, narratives of ontological difference, activating the site of 'creative strife' as the working through of 'truth' in this space. The artist crafted his materials through the inscriptions and the tools (*equipment*) used to inscribe, mould and form. Heidegger speaks of a *readiness-to-hand* in materials. They exist in concert with the act of making. In other words, they are working together, 'worlding the world': the artist, the tools and the equipment. It is not a question of an artist's mastery over matter: the equipment has a 'kind of being', a 'readiness to hand' (Heidegger 1927/1962, p. 98). The historicity

Figure 2: *Journey's Seed* by McInneny, Box Hill Melbourne. VicHealth Art and Environment Scheme, City of Whitehorse
Photographer: Nicholas Gresson 2005

of the materials, the 'equipmentality' works with the artist to let something new appear in the 'work-being' of the mirror-like forms and inscribed surfaces.

The work brings the locale, the tension between 'world' and 'earth', into being through its *techné*, conceived by the Greeks as 'producing, in terms of letting appear ... which brings something made, as something present, among the things that are already present' (Heidegger, 1999a; p. 361). Trees, trams, signs, lights, shops and shoppers are becoming present in the shiny metal surfaces as the forms fold and unfold in a 'letting appear' process: this the creative strife of world and earth. Heidegger (1999a), in 'Building Dwelling Thinking' speaks of the 'fourfold' occurring by dwelling in *earth, sky, mortals and divinities*. Does this include the urban space? Or must it be a 'natural' earth location of farm or countryside? Here is an often asked question relating to Heidegger's project: is he drawing from the nationalistic *Volk*, in essence, seeking a purity beyond a technological world as a return to a foundational concept of the German spirit? (Young, 1997).

In *The Political Ontology of Heidegger* (1991) Bourdieu suggests that an understanding of Heidegger's work comes from reconstructing the logic of the broader political and social forces of the Weimar Republic in early twentieth-century Europe. Beyond adopting any partisan position on Heidegger's philosophical or political genealogy with regard to the rise of the German Socialist party and Nazism, Bourdieu neither condemns nor redeems Heidegger. From this reading, one can adopt a clear understanding of the way texts are produced and the way their language orients itself in and through specific fields of social and political forces, with time and place both enacting forms of production.

As Julian Young (2001) puts it, citing Heidegger:

> The artwork, then, 'sets up' a world, brings it out of inconspicuousness and into salience, places it 'on display'. But it does not, says Heidegger, just do that. The setting up is not 'bare placing'. Rather, the work 'consecrates' its world, invests it with 'dignity and splendour', allows it to stand forth 'as holy' (*Poetry, Language, Thought*, p. 44). (Young, p. 38)

The viewers or passers-by, shoppers or commuters are as much a part of the urban place and the artwork as is the artist, the equipment and *Journey's Seed* itself. All together they disclose the spatial and temporal coordinates of their locale. It is here that the activation of *building* as *dwelling* takes place. Heidegger distinguishes between the 'work-being' and 'object-being' of artworks (1999b, p. 166). Beyond the codifications of the art industry and the artwork's commissioned value as a piece of public sculpture (a cultural production interpretation), *Journey's Seed* is set to work in 'the work-being of the work ... by way of the work's workly nature', in which there is a 'revealing' at work (Heidegger, 1999b, p. 165). There the working through of truth, *alētheia* happens: 'the truth of beings has set itself to work' (p. 165).

Thus the artwork occupies its site in an active ontology of difference disclosing its differential historicity of inception, making and future existence as a finite present. There is nothing passive here, nothing romantic and nothing disinterested. This is far removed from a Kantian universalised and necessarily purposive form of aesthetic judgement or Schopenhauer's aesthetic contemplation. Forgetfulness of *alētheia* has

15

meant that for too long Western philosophical systems have forgotten what it means 'to be'. In the later, 'Origin of the Work of Art' what Heidegger calls the 'thingly character of the thing' and 'the workly character of the work' becomes apparent, and there may be a possibility of remembering, not as memory, but as giving attention to being itself—*Being as it is lived in its experience of time*. Here, lies a call for remembering (through disclosure) the fundamental finiteness of Being in its differential ontology.

As Krell (1999c) reminds us, Heidegger shows that 'to think about building and dwelling appears to advance thought on the meaning of "Being"' (p. 345). Importantly, beyond aesthetic judgements and analysis of aesthetics as moral worth, this account activates an understanding of being human, in difference, in the world, and it is here, in the politics of difference, I find the pedagogical potential of Heidegger's project.

Bourdieu, Boyce and *Habitus*

How can Heidegger's 'letting-dwell' process draw alongside the concept of *habitus* as central to Bourdieu's project? Or is this an impossibility? French sociologist, Bourdieu proposed *habitus* as a generative set of dispositions in the inscribing of social attitudes and values. Such habits or competencies are transmitted in the home and through education, the dominant habits being transmitted by the dominant social class. This account, from the lineage of Norbert Elias and Max Weber, situates a system of schemas whereby certain practices are produced and reproduced as 'a system of lasting and transposable dispositions' (Bourdieu & Wacquant, 1992, p. 18). These dispositions are acquired via the conscious and unconscious processes of living in social environments and reproducing their values and practices. This includes aesthetics, which for Bourdieu is not accessed via the Kantian judgement of taste, but rather it is taste in cultural products and habits as produced, reproduced and made legitimate by a society's ruling classes: taste as a social construction (Bourdieu, 1986/1979).

Bourdieu was speaking of the class-based dispositions of symbolic or cultural capital that become embodied in one's life, times and institutional practices in such a way that their historical precedents are not readily available. They become apparent in the lived realities, practices, languages, laws and rules—and aesthetic values—of social institutions that amplify class-based distinctions. Bourdieu's *habitus* is '[t]he strategy-generating principle enabling agents to cope with the unforeseen and ever-changing situations' (Bourdieu & Wacquant, 1992, p. 18). Thus, human beings are active agents having effects upon the world of appearance, and the world in which these agents act is primarily one of economic and social conditions. Symbolic power relations are at work to compound cultural dispositions in institutions and individuals in a correlation of culture and social class. Such dispositions are reproducible through social practices. Thus, the public sphere for Bourdieu is a space of struggle to defend one's interests and positions through dominations of power, which are determining inclusions as symbolic capital and exclusions as a form of symbolic violence. In spite of a distancing from Heidegger, the site of struggle in Bourdieu's public space does contain traces of Heidegger's creative strife of earth and world, situated in the 'being-there' of *Dasein*.

Bourdieu does not seek to disturb the metaphysics of substance any more than Heidegger wants to consider cultural capital or dispositional dominance within the socius. Their lineages are different: one is ontological, the other epistemological. Bourdieu's 'epistemic reflexivity' is an epistemological project claiming a collective and objective framework in the sociology of knowledge.

We are Shipwrecked and Landlocked

Boyce's work, combining environmental and engineering geometries, is known for the mournful qualities it can evoke through references to empty urban parks and the inversion of outside into inside spaces. In 2008, Boyce was invited by John Kaldor to be the international artist in Australia in the Kaldor Public Art Projects. The institutional endorsement came from RMIT University providing the backing of resources and value recognition. Bourdieu's notion of *habitus* as a set of dispositions was evident through the workings of cultural institutions reproducing a dominant formation of élite value.

The constructional stage of installing *We are Shipwrecked and Landlocked* lasted a week in mid-October 2008, during which time there was an institutionally endorsed and funded roll-up of the recreational surface of artificial grass, which covered the heritage grounds of the Old Melbourne Gaol. This was followed by the digging of rectangular holes and placement of concrete footings at no more than 8 cm deep, to protect the heritage footings of the Gaol Courtyard. Finally, there was the erection of three aluminium trees, fabricated off-sight in Sydney and trucked down to Melbourne. Here was the construction of an artwork on a grand scale, akin to an engineering project in its technological necessities. Yet, the work was activating an aesthetic holding power with the trees' three to four m high geometries standing in contra-distinction to the worn bluestone of the adjacent Gaol. The trees were painted white on-site, and around them a fence of geometric design, painted black off-site, reflected the vocabulary of the tree structures and of a steel grating set into the ground—a drain to nowhere. Equidistant in each of three corners of the courtyard sat three, wire-mesh, rubbish bins, with copper tubing spray-painted yellow and draped through the fence to be left coiled on the ground near one of the trees suggesting a nonchalant emptiness. The final constructional act of building was to deliver and spread truckloads of granulated sand to emulate the unused, clay surface of the 'forgotten site' that had attracted the imagination of Boyce earlier in the year, prior to the university laying the artificial grass. The act of artifice was complete (Figure 3).

22 October 2008, saw the launch of *We are Shipwrecked and Landlocked* at an invitation event where, in Bourdieu's terms, the élite of art's social, cultural, institutional and intellectual worlds gathered to produce and reproduce their conditions of practice. The ensuing speeches, champagne and social discourse in the windswept locale gave witness to a relational field of forces: academic, art, media and business worlds coalesced in a dynamic matrix of material and aesthetic dispositions. This was a field of shared taste for an already endorsed artwork serving to reproduce a particular

Figure 3: Location of *We are Shipwrecked and Landlocked* by Boyce. Old Melbourne Gaol, RMIT Alumni Courtyard, Melbourne
Photographer: Nicholas Gresson 2008

aesthetic value. In this constructed world of appearances, made intelligible by transferrable dispositions and reproducible values, the socius was being inscribed by the symbolic forces of historical and political structures of *habitus*. The art world as an institution of society, writ large, was upholding its own values, and legitimating its own role in the socius. Here, the élite, educated classes were producing and reproducing their élite values through shared symbolic practices. In Bourdieu's terms, the élite values of cultural capital were inherently aesthetic, inherently violent, imposing their dominations upon the world.

Heidegger and Bourdieu in Application

The discussion is showing something of how the accounts of German philosopher, Heidegger, and French cultural sociologist, Bourdieu, provide two different interpretive procedures of art and aesthetics in urban space. The difference between the two is at the most fundamental level of metaphysics, to do with the human subject, and the relations of subjects and objects in the world. Bourdieu, as a structural sociologist coming from a Marxist tradition, works with objects and human subjects as social agents reinforcing underlying structures, with class as the organising principle of labour and capital. Bourdieu never pretends to dismantle the human subject as a pre-conditioned being or to displace the metaphysical world of appearances.

For Bourdieu, aesthetics is a matter of reproducible taste as élite value, conditioned and legitimated by class power in the banking and exchange of cultural capital. This process is implicitly operating in and through institutional agency, embedded in, and reproducing, the normative structures of society. On the other hand, Heidegger dismantles the preconditioned, metaphysics of presence in his account of the human subject and the world of things, displacing aesthetics along with rational accounts of appearances and *a priori* being.

Each account offers a way of recognising aesthetics and the struggle of being human in the world. Beyond, within, or in spite of, the structural circularity of social practices, the work of art as discussed with reference to the Millennium Bridge, McInneny and Boyce enacts a form of building as dwelling: this, an activating force at work as a Heideggerean site of disclosure. The artworks—and bridge—in their social and cultural sites of anchorage disclose the symbolic and cultural conditions of their 'work-being' as Heidegger put it, as they set to work the critical disputes characterising globalisation in terms of Bourdieu's reproducible dispositions. Within the differentiating processes of social space comprising the urban *habitus*, while remembering that Heidegger rejects the humanist tradition for its basis in metaphysics and its forgetting of being, 'we build and have built because we dwell, that is, because we are *dwellers*' (Heidegger, 1999a, p. 350, emphasis in original).

Pedagogical Gatherings as a Conclusion

The geometries of the Boyce trees enacted a strange disclosure of the locale that was otherwise overlooked too easily. As with the Millennium Bridge and *Journey's Seed*, there was a finite gathering as locale was brought into presence via an activation of questioning the meaning of aesthetics. Heidegger (1999a) would call this a summons to being: 'Rightly considered and kept well in mind, it is the sole summons that *calls* mortals into their dwelling' (p. 363, emphasis in original). Different approaches to talking about art as an activating practice by Heidegger and Bourdieu show how the work of art may open ontological, epistemological, cultural and political questions to do with being human in the world. The ontological force of Heidegger's enterprise meets the epistemological force of Bourdieu's. Both are political, but one is political in the sense of dismantling the politics of metaphysics, and the other is political in its way of exemplifying materialist norms within such politics.

Each enterprise when brought to the work of art activates questions about aesthetics, and through those questioning attitudes pedagogies of engagement may be possible. Perhaps, along with Bourdieu's *habitus*, Heidegger's ontological historicity could be 'abidingly in force' here. It is my belief that this relief of two significant thinkers activates pedagogy in the stratifications of history, cultural practices and philosophical logics of difference. The aim here is not to pit one philosophical enterprise against the other, but to see them 'dwell' in coexistence of difference; that is the politics within which this discussion seeks to work. Understanding the dominance of metaphysics within customary presence in which aesthetics finds a comfortable home, and displacing such dominance to find an 'otherwise' activation for objects or things in the world is, in itself, a pedagogy of earnest engagement.

Disclosure statement

No potential conflict of interest was reported by the author.

Notes

1. McInneny is an urban artist lecturing in public art at the School of Art, RMIT University and is undertaking a PhD with the RMIT School of Architecture and Design. He lives in Melbourne, and is a member of Architects for Peace.
2. Boyce was educated at Glasgow School of Art, graduating with MA in 1997, and lives in Scotland. He won the 2011 Turner Art Prize.
3. The bridge was completed in 2001. It won the 2002 Royal Institute of British Architects (RIBA) Stirling Prize.
4. See Heidegger *Being and Time* (1927/1962).
5. Baumgarten introduced the term 'aesthetics' in his *Meditationes Philosophicae denonnullis ad poema* (1735) [Philosophical meditations pertaining to some matters concerning poetry].
6. See Beardsley (1958, 1969 and 1982), Dickie (1965, 1974 and 1987).
7. See further discussion of Heidegger and the work of art in Grierson (2008).
8. *Journey's Seed* was commissioned by VicHealth. Architects for Peace, Retrieved 25 September 2014 from http://studio-space.blogspot.com/2005/07/journeys-seed.html.

References

Architects for Peace. (2011). Journey's seed, studio + space project gallery, blogspot. Retrieved 25 September, 2014, from http://studio-space.blogspot.com/2005/07/journeys-seed.html
Beardsley, M. C. (1958). *Aesthetics*. Indianapolis, IN: Hackett.

Beardsley, M. C. (1969). Aesthetic experience regained. *The Journal of Aesthetics and Art Criticism, 28*, 3–11.

Beardsley, M. C. (1982). *The aesthetic point of view*. Ithaca, NY: Cornell University Press.

Bourdieu, P. (1977/1972). *Outline of a theory of practice*. (R. Nice, Trans.). Cambridge: Cambridge University Press.

Bourdieu, P. (1986/1979). *Distinction: A social critique of the judgement of taste*. (R. Nice, Trans.). London: Routledge & Kegan Paul.

Bourdieu, P. (1990/1980). *The logic of practice*. Cambridge: Polity Press.

Bourdieu, P. (1991). *The political ontology of Martin Heidegger*. Stanford, CA: Stanford University Press.

Bourdieu, P., & Wacquant, L. J. D. (1992). *An invitation to reflexive sociology*. Cambridge: Polity Press.

Boyce, M. (2008). *We are shipwrecked and landlocked*. Public art installation, RMIT University, Alumni Courtyard, 22 October–30 November.

Dickie, G. (1964). The myth of the aesthetic attitude. *American Philosophical Quarterly, 1*, 56–65.

Dickie, G. (1965). Beardsley's phantom aesthetic experience. *The Journal of Philosophy, 62*, 129–136.

Dickie, G. (1974). *Art and the aesthetic: An institutional analysis*. Ithaca, NY: Cornell University Press.

Dickie, G. (1987). *Evaluating art*. Philadelphia, PA: Temple University Press.

Dickie, G. (1997). *Introduction to aesthetics: An analytic approach*. Oxford: Oxford University Press.

Findlay, J. N. (1977). Foreword. In Hegel, G. W. F. (1977/1807). *Phenomenology of spirit*. (A. V. Miller, Trans., pp. v–xxx). Oxford: Oxford University Press.

Grierson, E. (2008). Heeding Heidegger's way: Questions of the work of art. In Karalis, V. (Ed.), *Heidegger and the aesthetics of living* (pp. 45–64). Cambridge: Cambridge Scholars Press.

Guignon, C. (Ed.). (2006). *The Cambridge companion to Heidegger* (2nd ed.). Cambridge: Cambridge University Press.

Hegel, G. W. F. (1977/1807). *Phenomenology of spirit*. (A. V. Miller, Trans.). Oxford: Oxford University Press.

Hegel, G. W. F. (1993/1886). *Introductory lectures on aesthetics*. (B. Bosanquet, Trans.). London: Penguin Books.

Heidegger, M. (1927/1962). *Being and time*. (J. Macquarrie & E. Robinson, Trans.). Oxford: Blackwell.

Heidegger, M. (1977). The question concerning technology. In (W. Lovitt, Trans.), *The question concerning technology and other essays* (pp. 3–35). New York, NY: Harper & Row.

Heidegger, M. (1999a). Building dwelling thinking. In D. Krell (Ed.), *Basic writings: Martin Heidegger* (pp. 343–363). London: Routledge.

Heidegger, M. (1999b). The origin of the work of art. In D. Krell (Ed.), *Basic writings: Martin Heidegger* (pp. 139–212). London: Routledge.

Heidegger, M. (1999c). Letter on humanism. In D. Krell (Ed.), *Basic writings: Martin Heidegger* (pp. 213–265). London: Routledge.

Krell, D. (1999a). General introduction. The question of being. In D. Krell (Ed.), *Basic writings: Martin Heidegger* (pp. 1–35). London: Routledge.

Krell, D. (1999b). Introduction to the origin of the work of art. In D. Krell (Ed.), *Basic writings: Martin Heidegger* (pp. 140–142). London: Routledge.

Krell, D. (1999c). Introduction to building dwelling thinking. In D. Krell (Ed.), *Basic writings: Martin Heidegger* (pp. 344–346). London: Routledge.

Krell, D. (Ed.). (1999d). *Basic writings: Martin Heidegger*. London: Routledge.

McInneny, A. (2005). *Journey's seed*. Melbourne: Box Hill, Public art Installation.

Young, J. (1997). *Heidegger, philosophy, Nazism*. Cambridge, MA: Cambridge University Press.

Young, J. (2001). *Heidegger's philosophy of art*. Cambridge: Cambridge University Press.

Rendering Visible: Painting sexuate ontologies

LINDA DALEY

Abstract

In this essay, I examine Luce Irigaray's aesthetic of sexual difference, which she develops by extrapolating from Paul Klee's idea that the role of painting is to render the non-visible rather than represent the visible. This idea is the premise of her analyses of phenomenology and psychoanalysis and their respective contributions to understanding art and sexual identity. I claim that Irigaray assembles an aesthetic of sexual difference that exceeds these familiar intellectual traditions, one that articulates the encounter of non-visible, material (human and non-human) forces that engender modes of sexuate being and becoming. I further claim that this encounter is the very matter of artistry and art-making.

Is not art a means of creating reality and not only of reproducing it?

Art is a daily task for each one of us, and sexuate belonging is the most crucial dimension that art has to work out. (Irigaray, 2004c, p. 97)

Section 1

In a piece of art criticism rarely found in her body of work, feminist philosopher Luce Irigaray makes a negative judgement on the German surrealist writer and visual artist, Unica Zürn (1916–1970), claiming that she 'fail[s] to be born' as both a woman and an artist (1994, p. 13). According to the philosopher, Zürn's paintings and drawings depict a negative relation to herself and the world: as a formless 'other' to man. Zürn's art, including autobiographical accounts of her relation with artist partner Hans Bellmer, reveals the psychic pain that in moments of reprieve provided material for her art, but also led to her suicide. For Irigaray, Zürn's art encapsulates her theories of woman's deadly relation to patriarchy. Although Irigaray defends her statements by claiming they are not directed at the artist, but rather raise questions about art, the disclaimer did not convince her English translator, Margaret Whitford (1994, p. 12). The feminist scholar and translator made a reply to the piece in a subsequent issue of the art journal, noting Irigaray's value to practising artists as a philosopher, but as a critic, having little to offer. Art critic, Hilary Robinson added to the exchange by reaffirming Irigaray's value to practising artists and by taking both the philosopher and Whitford to task for privileging a literary model in assessing the artist's work that failed to consider the materials and techniques with which the visual artist worked (1995, p. 20). To my knowledge, Irigaray has not ventured into art criticism since the Zürn piece. However, she has continued to write on art practices, and on the relation of colour to painting in ways that are rich and productive for thinking difference for artists and non-artists alike. I draw attention to this curious moment in Irigaray studies because it captures a problem with one philosopher that reflects a problem for feminist aesthetics more broadly.

Feminist aesthetics is a fraught area of inquiry. For much of the past several decades, it has succumbed to at least two familiar divisions: between art and politics on the one hand, and for longer than several decades, between art and philosophy on the other (Grosz, 2008; Ziarek, 2012). With the first of these divisions, feminist aesthetics had arrived at a position of either subordinating the work's specificity to its political value, or overly focusing on the formal qualities of the work to ignore the forms and conditions of power that inflect the production and reception of the work. With the division between art and philosophy, the art work's expressive and affective power has often been silenced by the explanatory and evaluative power of philosophy by way of the traditional aesthetic categories of style, taste, autonomy and genius, among others. Whether by assuming these terms are gender neutral or able to be corrected by feminist perspectives, philosophy has traditionally positioned itself as the voice of the work speaking for its assumed mute and passive existence. Effectively, this is the position Irigaray occupied with Unica Zürn's work, and which Whitford—and possibly Irigaray upon reflection—reject. The consequence of these divisions has led to a situation of retreat by feminist theorists. Rita Felski, for example, claims that the project of feminist aesthetics is doomed because irrespective of the artistic medium, it presumes a normative aesthetic (1995, p. 431). Felski calls for feminist theorising to 'go beyond feminist aesthetics, but not by ignoring the realm of the aesthetic' (1995, p. 431).

How might philosophy and art make a mutual encounter in ways that do not succumb to the impasses of the past? Should feminism rely less on aesthetics—as the branch of philosophy that traditionally participates in the domain of art—to instead consider non-aesthetic concepts and philosophical approaches to art to activate the 'realm of the aesthetic?' And would that be an aesthetic still? I approach these questions by returning to other of Irigaray's writings on art and sexual difference to consider how non-aesthetic concepts and contexts can contribute to a philosophy of art compatible with feminist aims; one that offers generative potential for professional artists as well as the everyday artistry of being-in-the-world.

In the several, and sometimes cryptic, remarks Irigaray makes about colour and its necessary (although by no means exclusive) relation to painting, I locate Irigaray's aesthetic of sexual difference. I argue that Irigaray's references to painting have nothing to do with critiques of representations of women *in* art as rather her turning towards the painter's task to think through the materiality of their medium, one that is analogous to philosophy's problem in thinking sexual difference. Before I address the status of art and painting in her writing, I turn to her concept of sexual difference.

Section 2

Irigaray explicitly rejects the label 'feminist' to describe her theoretical aims, preferring women's, and more so, humanity's liberation (See Irigaray, 2002a, p. 67). Central to her idea of liberation is the concept of sexual difference, an ontological category constitutively philosophical, political and ethical (Grosz, 2012, p. 70). Sexual difference is not only the organising concept in her philosophy; it is also the philosophical problem of our era par excellence (1993b, p. 5). Conventional accounts explaining the differences between the sexes do so according to one of three typical models: where women and the feminine are either opposite, complementary or equal to men and the masculine. By contrast, sexual difference as Irigaray accounts for, is premised on a notion of difference where the terms woman/man; women/men; feminine/masculine do not pre-exist their difference and do not invoke a hierarchy between the terms. Irigaray says 'who or what the other is, I never know. But the other who is forever unknowable is the one who differs from me sexually' (1993b, p. 13). 'She' is different from 'he' in a mode that is of another order to the difference 'he' is from 'she': the difference is non-reciprocal as well as non-hierarchical. It is a model of difference based on two sexes that are irreducible to each other.

Irigaray's term 'sexuate' describes a positively defined feminine identity that does not currently exist within patriarchy and phallocentrism. It refers to the bodily, psychical and cultural dimensions of feminine (and implicitly masculine) being that for woman is reconceived from her negative and sexually neutral status within phallocentrism to a positive, sexually different status. 'Sexuate' refers not simply to anatomical or genital differences between men and women (although it does include these and what they enable) as if this difference were some kind of essence to sexual identity or a grounding principle of sexual being. It incorporates a transfigured conception of a being's identity that comprises dimensions that are *morphological* (bodily in the widest sense of a living form), *perceptual* (in terms of the sensate perspective a sexed being has of self, others and the world) and *associative* qualities (the kinds of relations that are possible for sexually different beings) (Grosz, 2012, p. 70). These dimensions of being relational, bodily and perspectival override the possibility of reducing Irigaray's account of sexual difference as biologically essentialist or heterosexist. In Irigaray's more recent writings, she speaks of the productive encounter between sexuate beings involving the creation of a third being, which cannot be reduced to the production of a child, nor a privileging of the heterosexual couple: 'the real exists as at least three: a real corresponding to the masculine subject, a real corresponding to the feminine subject, and a real corresponding to their relation. These three reals thus each correspond to a world, but these three worlds are in interaction' (2002b, p. 111). Some feminists of difference have read Irigaray's work subsequent to her early and predominantly critical philosophical interventions as regressively heterosexist (Butler, Cornell, Cheah, & Grosz, 1998). However, Irigaray is explicit in not reducing the couple to a familial

unit of reproduction: 'Maternity—giving birth to a child—should remain an extra …
surplus to any morphology' (1994, p. 13).

Sexual difference is real, but it is not reality. It is a difference that does not accord
with any existent identity or term. The ontological dynamic of a being's identity, as a
mode of becoming that Irigaray's concept necessitates, is not permissible under the
Aristotelian logic of ontology that needs being to be either A or not-A. Within this
logic, a being is defined according to a grouping of dominant characteristics comprising its identity/term as a universal category (A), or according to the absence of those
(other being's) characteristics in order for this being to belong to a universal identity
foreign to its singularity (not-A). For Irigaray, sexuate being is a mode of becoming
other than how feminine identity is defined according to this dominant logic, by
becoming in different moments of encounter with self and other through the various
dimensions of woman's (and implicitly man's) singularly sexuate being.

Irigarayan sexuate difference, then, and the culture of worlds that it would make
possible, is a radically transformed understanding of conventional ways of thinking
who and what we are as beings, and the nature of our relations to each other and the
world. She seeks methods, techniques and practices, along with concepts, with which
to think that expression. In addition to the philosophical tradition (among other traditions), Irigaray turns to painters and to painting to begin the transformations required
to be thought and practised by sexuate difference. How, for example, does the visual
medium of painting afford techniques, methods and approaches that give expression
to what not only does not exist in reality, but must also of necessity remain 'forever
unknowable?' What do modernist painters' preoccupation with vision and perception
offer to Irigaray's philosophy? How does the material of colour, its handling and
applications—unique to each painter—participate in making visible the *invisible* sensations in the encounter between sexuate subjects that is yet to happen, and of which
Irigaray describes as a 'field of forces' the two sexes generate (2002b, p. 108).

Before turning to these questions, we need to consider the necessity of transforming
the relations of form to matter and of space to time to see the relevancy to the task of
painting sexuate difference. First, is the reconfiguration of the logic of form and matter. Irigaray has analysed the traditional relation in Western thought of matter to form
and its sexual *indifference* to woman through her critique of the place of fluids within
theories of solids. Phallocentrism requires that what is counted as real has to conform
to a logic which reflects the morphological qualities of the masculine sex ('production,
property, order, form, unity, visibility, erection') (1985b, p. 77). Fluids are analogous
to woman's subjectivity within this patriarchal logic: woman, like fluids, cannot be
counted as real or having a reality of her own that can be formalised on her own
terms because the real of her being, like that of fluids, is of another order of logic to
that of phallocentrism and its discourses of symbolisation. Irigaray reminds us that
ontology presumes (a) form that gives a shape, dimension(s) and substance to matter,
and therefore presumes a logic of relation between the matter/material of what is
(contained) within its form. The analogy between the resistance to formalisation of
fluidity with woman's being is that the universal, abstracted logic unifying reality
which underpins phallocentrism refuses the 'indefinite and the in-finite *form* [that] is
never complete' in her being (1985a, p. 229). Fluidity, like solids, names physical

reality and includes internal frictions, pressures and movements 'continuous, compressible, dilatable, viscous, conductible, diffusible ... unending, potent and impotent owing to its resistance to the countable' (1985c, p. 111). Fluids participate within, across and through the walls of solids; they are not contained by the logic that erects the 'solid/fluid' hierarchical pairing, and undermine that opposition in fluids' refusal to be in one *or* other place, conforming to one *or* other form. As fluids are to theories of mechanics, so too is woman's being to symbolisation within the phallocentric morphologic: woman's form is not one. Woman does not belong to *a* form that would be geometrically placed in space and mathematically countable like the solid object in space.

Irigaray links her critique of the dominant logic of forms to colour. In ways that are analogous to fluids and fluidity, colour participates in Irigaray's philosophy because, as Ludwig Wittgenstein reminds us, conceptually, colour is in excess of any attempt to order its physical reality to a system or schema (n.d., p. 16e). The patriarchal forms in which women have always existed are inappropriate to feminine identity, and, says Irigaray, we must break out of them through 'acts of liberation' which may enable us to discover colour ... what's left of life beyond forms ... When all meaning is taken away from us, there remains color, colors, in particular, those corresponding to our sex ... (1993c, p. 109). Ontologically, colour has multiple forms of affectivity both natural and cultural that are transformative: for example, in animal and plant life, forms that enable attractions and repulsions within and across species; in the spiritual domain of some cultures showing relations between inside and outside (Irigaray's example refers to the role of chakras in the practice of yoga), and it has forms in painting that are transformations of relations between perceptual and pictorial space, and in rendering visible and non-visible forces. Colour does not conform to quantity and abstraction, the mathematisation of Aristotelian logic. Rather, it is pure quality. Irigaray, therefore, looks to art, artists and art practices to find forms and transformations with colour, and the thinking that painters have brought to their material.

Second, Irigaray seeks the reconfiguration of space to time. A sexuate culture requires a change in our understanding of perception and of the inhabiting of place so that femininity is not figured as space, and masculinity is figured as time as they are under patriarchy and phallocentrism (1993b, p. 7; see also Olkowski, 2000). Woman must not be figured as space for man to achieve his accession to subjectivity and thus to history, and woman must not be outside her internal and external relations to time and thus figured as what history cannot admit *as woman* (Irigaray, 2002b, pp. 121–122). Woman needs a place proper to herself by having a limit or point of return within herself, and in not being the place of limit for man as she is within patriarchy. To achieve this rethinking of the 'whole economy of space-time', and the relation of matter to form, Irigaray must look to the resources both within and outside philosophy for the reconfiguration of sexed being to take place (1993b, p. 11).

Section 3

One of Irigaray's most important influences for thinking sexual difference beyond dualist structures by way of embodied existence is Maurice Merleau-Ponty, who is unique among the early phenomenologists in aiming to get 'to the things themselves' in a pre-reflective manner via the perceiving body. His philosophy relies heavily on painters to advance and illustrate such that Irigaray says it 'almost mistakes itself for a phenomenology of painting or of the art of painting' (1993b, p. 175). Given that woman has traditionally been on the subordinate side of dualist thinking—mind/body; spirit/flesh; subject/object—the phenomenologist's philosophy contributes much in the development of her own.

Merleau-Ponty pays close attention to René Descartes's views on painting and its relation to colour in inaugurating his philosophy away from Cartesian 'operationalism' claiming it assumes pre-reflective contact with a 'tacit cogito' which his phenomenology targets (1962, p. 402). For Descartes, colour had been understood as a secondary quality to the quantity of *res extensa*, and contributes to the simulacra detrimental and redundant to representation. Like other inessential sensory qualities, colour has laws that are inaccessible to vision, and vision for Descartes is dominant among the senses. Although vision depends on colour to make the discriminations worthy of its place in the sensorium, for the early modern metaphysician, colour judgements will lead to error. The percipient views colour as inhering in the property of the thing rather than in a relation between the percipient and the perceived. Descartes's optics also views vision as passive and cannot account for the optical laws of colour perception: light and colour are signs instituted by nature to which humans do not have the code to read its laws. Descartes's expressed preference for the (non-coloured) graphic arts to that of painting, encapsulates for the phenomenologist the monochrome and machine-like model of techno-rationalist thinking that dominates all dimensions of his metaphysics in its grasping, mastering and objectifying operations of rationalist thought. As colour is ontologically essential for painting, for Merleau-Ponty it cannot be treated as a mere secondary quality, and has instead the capacity of 'leading us somewhat closer to "the heart of things"'; that is, to that pre-reflective contact with being (1993b, p. 141).

Merleau-Ponty focuses on how post-impressionist Paul Cézanne, (in his writings as well as his paintings), is able to create a modulation of relations between things on the canvas, not by giving priority to line that would contain the thing within a determined form. Rather, the artist creates a form that is achieved through giving representation on the canvas to a mode of pre-reflective or 'lived' perceptions that are prior to the perception that consciousness organises into a perceptual unity of objects in a spatial field (1993a, p. 64). Cézanne's thought and practice is applauded by Merleau-Ponty on two counts. First, in representing on the canvas a way of seeing the world so that the contour or form of the thing is rendered as it emerges to our vision. As Merleau-Ponty says: 'Cézanne follows the swelling of the object ... one's glance captures a shape that emerges from among them all, just as it does in perception' (1993a, p. 65). Cézanne's canvas depicts the practically imperceptible movement of the various phenomenological dimensions of lived perception. It is the perceptual experience as 'lived' in its immediacy with and immersion in the world that intertwines seer with seen. Of his art, Merleau-Ponty says: 'in reality we see a form which oscillates around the ellipse without being an ellipse' (1993a, p. 64). The pictorial effect is not a thing presented as a single outline sacrificing the thing's depth, but rather a thing that is presented as 'an inexhaustible reality full of reserves' (1993a, p. 65) Second, Merleau-Ponty admires Cézanne for perfecting a method for achieving that movement of pre-reflective perceptual vision through the modulation of colours and their relations on the canvas. The priority Cézanne gives to colour (over line) results in colour blurring with line making the two painterly resources dissolve in order to achieve a spatial structure that 'vibrates' in the thing's representation on the canvas. In that 'vibration', says Merleau-Ponty, 'we see the depth, the smoothness, the softness, the hardness of objects ... the presence ... which for us is the definition of the real' (1993a, p. 65). The painter's thought and practice achieves a method for pictorial space that has its parallel in what Merleau-Ponty is seeking phenomenologi-cally: a tactile sense of vision; a mode of vision that is chiasmically rather than dualis-tically understood as the embodied relation of a self to the world.

In Merleau-Ponty's idea of 'the flesh', he conceives a more primordial formulation of embodied perception understood as the condition of both seeing and being seen, and of touching and being touched (1968, p. 147). Sight and touch have a fundamen-tal and necessary interaction for perception, and they are common to, and the condi-tion of, both the subject and the object in being a single 'thing' folded back on itself (1968, p. 147). Again, the ontology of colour is crucial to the phenomenologist's pro-ject to undermine dualist structures of thought. To use Merleau-Ponty's example: the Red is seen and felt as a 'certain differentiation, an ephemeral modulation of this world—less a colour or a thing, therefore, than the difference between things and col-ours, a momentary chrystallisation of coloured being or visibility' (1968, p. 132). The red separates from, to continue his example, the dress, to connect with other reds that neighbour it, and form a constellation or field of reds that gives, in another moment of sensation, the dress in its form as thing-like and ultimately as object. His concept of the flesh is an element of being with the capacity to fold in on itself, to face inward towards the self, as well as outward towards other things and beings, and to express the sensation of being as it is lived. His example of the double sensation of one hand touching and being touched by the other in a single fold of two hands illustrates this inward and outward interfaces of the modulations connecting and reversing subject and object, whereby a body can be both and at once subject and object within the same field of visibility (1968, p. 134). The flesh expresses the shimmering or quiver-ing of the visual sense felt on the eye as the difference that connects and disconnects colour to and from the thing. More so than any other element in his account of the flesh, colour has an ontological status for Merleau-Ponty of being the 'exemplar sensi-ble' in that it both gives itself as a being, and is the condition of Being (1968, p. 135).

In spite of his philosophy's advance beyond dualist, mechanistic subjectivity, Irigaray's several engagements with his philosophy demonstrate how his phenomenol-ogy still retains the domination of vision within the sensorium through a reliance on maternal and feminine metaphors of experience, but does so while ignoring the real of women's bodies. Woman's maternal and feminine elements of her being, compli-cate his phenomenology of the flesh, which ultimately maintains a monosexual con-ception of embodiment and of the flesh's relation to the world (1993b, p. 177). Irigaray begins her critique of the phenomenologist's monosexual philosophy in her chapter, 'The Invisible of the Flesh: A Reading of Merleau-Ponty's *The Visible and the Invisible*, "The Intertwining—The Chiasm"' in *An Ethics of Sexual Difference* (1993b), develops it further in 'Flesh Colors' in *Sexes and Genealogies* (1993a) and again in 'To Paint the Invisible' (2004b). Irigaray is critical of Merleau-Ponty's references to feminine attributes such as fluidity (through metaphors such as 'between the sea and the strand'); references to female desire (with the comment: 'the telepathy of the visible when a woman knows her body to be desirable without even seeing those who look at her'); and to woman's body ('Pregnancy, *Gestalt*, phenomenon—represent a getting into contact with being as pure *there is*' (1968, p. 245; 206). While pregnancy is the word for Merleau-Ponty that 'gives' the pure givenness of the *there is*, he overlooks the particular entwinement of the flesh of the maternal body and its complication to his theory of visibility and invisibility in the relation between mother and fetus. His references to the red of the woman's dress ignores the more primordial red of her blood, let alone the white of her milk, or the colour of the fetus's eyes that have a different relation again to the light and to the inside and outside of a field of sensation (Irigaray, 1993b, p. 156).

Merleau-Ponty's claim of reversibility of sight and touch may work for man but, says Irigaray, not so readily for woman. The experience of tactility for and between the fetus and the mother is not a relation of reversibility that he proposes, and in terms of the senses' reversibility, it is likewise not of the order of symmetry in that mother and fetus have a relation to their lived experience of spatiality *vis a vis* each other that is not reducible to sight (Irigaray, 1993b, p. 160). In the maternal relation, tactility has more of a relation to the sense of hearing than to vision (Irigaray, 1993b, p. 160). To Merleau-Ponty's hand-touching-hand allegory of the reversible positioning of active and passive sensation, Irigaray proposes the two lips where one is not dominant and grasping by one of the other, but remains in constant intimacy and is in woman's body, already doubled sensation (1993b, p. 167).

The world that Merleau-Ponty describes as symbiotic with a sensible self, Irigaray describes as 'solitary and solipsistic:' an inward and outward movement of a masculine subject that forgets the prior movement of symbiosis of fetus and placenta (2004b, p. 394). From Irigaray's perspective, Merleau-Ponty's conception of world is a substitute for the even more primordial realm of the placenta, the sensible realm to which all human beings have a relation as the first 'lived experience' of co-belonging and co-existing. The placenta is an organ that undertakes an intermediating role between mother and fetus by performing functions that benefit both beings while also being relatively autonomous of each: supplying blood and nutrients to the fetus and secreting hormones to the mother ceased by the ovaries during gestation (1993c, p. 39). Unlike the current cultural imaginary of the fetus as *either* fused with the mother *or* as a foreign body cannibilising its host, the biological reality of the placenta is a prized sensible-transcendental term (invisible/visible in Merleau-Ponty's) for rethinking the intermediation of the third being of sexuate identities.

Irigaray's relation to Merleau-Ponty's philosophy is highly equivocal yet she does not repudiate phenomenology even when questioned about its value to her work (Irigaray, 2008, pp. 129–132). Rather, she adapts the concept of 'the flesh' to other contexts such as the clinical practice of psychoanalysis and destabilises both practice and theory and the relation between the two. Irigaray's relation to psychoanalysis is similarly highly equivocal, however, she has been a practicing psychoanalyst herself and views psychoanalysis as having the potential for transformation because it is the 'scene that calls the very condition of representation into question' (2002c, p. 193). Irigaray considers the 'drama of analysis' as theatrical in its incorporation of the physical props, gestures or the bodily posture(s) of its actors, and the verbal and non-verbal exchanges of speaker/listener: a setting that 'corresponds to an optical illusion' (2002c, p. 199, 201). She argues the classical setting of the encounter creates an artificial reality that places the analysand in a 'blind' and 'supine' orientation towards the analyst and therefore disoriented from her immediate, and particularly, visual perceptions. The sensory deprivation of both actors is further described in terms of the disequilibrium of sound and light waves affecting the analysand's perceptual capacities.

In 'Flesh Colors', Irigaray prescribes to her colleagues (the essay was originally delivered as a lecture to a professional conference) that the solution to this disequilibrium between the non-human speeds of light and sound forces and the disorientation between human actors is 'to paint'. Her point is not only to reorientate the position of the actors (side-by-side and vertical rather than back-to-front and vertical/horizontal) in the encounter. Her aim is also to provide another form to the expression of those perceptual affects through a non-linguistic medium. Irigaray claims that the different speeds of light and sound (waves) are the conditions of vision and hearing (that is, conditions of the perceptual field) between subjects, but the different speeds of this 'physical matter' of real, invisible and non-human forces puts speech/listening out of balance, and leads to the analysand's inability to integrate the present in the past, and the past into the present and the future. Irigaray says: 'we need to give back to each sense the objective and subjective speeds of its current perceptions and facilitate harmony between these, and the past, present, and future history of the subject' (1993a, p. 156).

Citing Paul Klee, she says that painting in the therapeutic encounter would 'spatialize perception and make time simultaneous' (1993a, 155). Against Freud's (untheorised) *practice* of the 'talking cure' and his *theory* of the death drive (that women fail to sublimate) as the necessary prerequisite for a transition to culture, Irigaray overlays these Freudian insights with Merleau-Ponty's phenomenology to radically surpass both knowledge domains. And painting is the key to her strategy.

Freud examines sublimation of the death drives in a number of places in his writings, but it is his connection of the subject's psychical processes to the founding of social organization that has relevance to Irigaray's imperative that women must learn 'the art of genital sublimation' (1993a, p. 165). Sublimation is a psychical process consisting of the abandonment of an erotic aim and taking on another that is social. Freud argues that ability to sublimate bodily drives and their manifestation in affects, representations and artistic practices is the source of human civilization and creativity (1961, p. 82). Without this ability, he says, we lose the basis for creating meaning for our own lives, and we remain unhappy or outside culture. Freud offers some suggestions for overcoming the arbitrariness of the opportunity to sublimate, such as devoting one's life to artistic production. Freud claims that for human civilisation to appear, mankind's sexual desire must be redirected from two natural aims: the body of the mother and the bodies of men. When the desire engendered among men, by urinating on the threatening flames of fire, was redirected to another aim, culture came into being. The continued sublimation of both incestuous and homosexual desire would ensure culture's progression. Freud claims that due to women's anatomical deficiency for dousing the flames, her role was to be the guardian of the fire. In Freudian theory, then, woman's genitals represent a double handicap in being neither beautiful nor culturally productive, merely *re*-productive. To which Irigaray replies:

> This imperative of genital sublimation [something that we women have either forgotten or never learned the art of] solves the dilemma of art for art's sake. If art is a necessary condition for the establishment of a culture of affective relationships, and especially sexual relationships, then art is useful as a place where individual, bodily matter can be transmuted and sublimated. Art is not just an aid to a social body that has already been abstracted from the sexual dimension ... Without art, sexuality falls into a natural immediacy that is bound up with reproduction and into infinite particles. (1993a, p. 165)

We know from Merleau-Ponty that colour can be a mode of access to 'pre-discursive experience' and that for him painting unlike drawing is a mode of expression more appropriate to making intelligible that sensible experience than is the mode of spoken language (Irigaray, 1993b, p. 151). It is also an expression which produces in the psychoanalytic clinical encounter an artefact shared with another that may be ephemeral or enduring, but one that would contribute to thinking a *sexuate* culture in the way in which Freud speaks of artistic activity as a necessity of culture's founding and perpetuation. Given that woman's role in monosexual economies of culture have been caught between her value as a use and as an exchange—as a value of utility even when she is a sign of value—the production of a woman-defined culture through the creation of non-utilitarian production of art would seem to be a necessary precondition of Irigaray's *sexuate* culture (see Daley, 2012).

Irigaray directs her complex reading of intersubjectivity and sexual identity in 'Flesh Colors' through painting in the clinical context. She is also making a larger claim for women's creativity to the construction or production of a culture appropriate to her sex: 'This is the indispensable road to take not only for psychoanalysis but, more generally, in every relationship, if we are to realize an art of the sexual that respects the colors, the sounds, and the forms proper to each sex' (1993a, p. 165).

In 'To Paint the Invisible', Irigaray spells out the role of painting and the painter that she had begun in her earlier essays as more explicitly a relation to invisibility. Drawing out the understanding of the monosexual invisibility in Merleau-Ponty's philosophy, Irigaray refines her understanding of its role for her own enterprise. Alphonso Lingis, translator of *The Visible and the Invisible*, explains the invisible as the 'wild *Logos*' that does not constitute a set of principles or laws, but rather a system of levels posited in the sensible field by our body (1968, p. li). The invisible offers a cognitive unity or the intelligibility by means of which sensible things are distributed in a field according to proximity or distance, and differentiated according to qualities or intensities. He adds: 'like the light, these levels and dimensions [of the sensible], this system of lines of force, are not *what* we see; they are that *with which, according to which, we see'* (Lingis, 1968, p. li). The invisible is the field that unfolds the visible of sensible being.

Again in reference to Paul Klee, whose well-known formula: *the painter's task is not to render the visible as rather render visible,* Irigaray refines her account of what constitutes the invisibility of the flesh for sexual difference, and implicates the role of painting in its actualisation. Whereas, in her chapter in *An Ethics of Sexual Difference,* Irigaray names the invisible as the maternal-feminine, elsewhere she refers to the invisible as 'relations between us and the world, us and the other(s)' (1993b, p. 173, 2004a, p. 395). Irigaray progressively refines her understanding of the invisible of sexuate difference from terms that do not exist in the imaginary and symbolic orders to terms for expressing the ontological real of woman and of her series of relations that are constitutive of her being and for which she seeks forms that do not yet exist. The current phase of Irigaray's writings comes to increasingly focus on real forces that are non-human and inorganic in comprising the contours of these relations to the world (s) in which we co-belong. These worlds are of another order of relation to the single world Merleau-Ponty's flesh outlines (see Irigaray, 2013, 2002b, 2004b). The ethical dimension of her ontology of sexual difference therefore expands the ontology of her ethics beyond any bodily limit of 'lived experience' [*Erlebnis*] of phenomenological inquiry. Irigaray says: 'the ability to be at the same time seeing and seen, touching and touched, does not seem to be specifically human' (2004b, p. 397). The 'specifically human' is insufficient for defining relations with the world and others, or sufficient in characterising 'becoming human' (Irigaray, 2002b, pp. 117–133). In 'Flesh Colors,' Irigaray describes these non-human forces of the real on sexed beings in reference to the invisible forces of light waves and sound waves in producing the perceptual field prior to the language in which perceptions would be interpreted. Furthermore, these forces have different affective modalities on the perceptual capacities of the subjects according to their sex (2004b, p. 397). Irigaray folds back Merleau-Ponty's thought onto itself seeking not so much to preserve his conception of a flesh that materially provides the support for both vision and thought, but of opening 'another relation between flesh, vision and thought' (2004b, p. 390).

Irigaray is critical of Freud for his theory of sublimation, in refusing women the access to the creation of culture, she is also critical of Freudian theory that forgot its early practice as 'talking cure' when the analyst listened closely to what women were saying and how they were saying it (2002a, p. 208). At a certain historical point in its development as a science, psychoanalysis forgot to listen to women's voices (2002a, p. 203). Significantly, Irigaray is not urging a return to that early kind of listening, as rather a different mode of encounter between analyst and analysand: a sexually different relation to the perceptual field; a sexually different orientation of bodies in the analytical field; and a non-linguistic mode of expression that has an essential relation to colour.

Section 4

We might ask of Irigaray's aesthetic, Why painting? Why is her reconfigured aesthetic focused on the resources of an art form that among all the arts, is possibly the most inherently misogynist in its traditional figuring of woman as muse to the genius (male) artist or as the model of beauty to be represented; where the studio is a physical exter-nalisation of the appropriation of place that Irigaray's analyses repeatedly examine and repudiate (see Pollock, 1992; Schor, 1997)? Why painting rather than, say, writ-ing, sculpture or music? First, painting has an ontological link with colour in a way that, as we have seen via Merleau-Ponty and Descartes, other forms of rendering do not. Second, as Irigaray reminds us, colour belongs to nature as well as to culture, and her philosophy seeks methods and techniques for thinking the contexts of their reconnection. Third, since the crisis in representation that photography's arrival cre-ated more than one and a half centuries ago, it is painting's task to render visible what is otherwise imperceptible or invisible. Rendering the invisible of sexuate subjectivity and culture is Irigaray's aim. It also marks the tension that her philosophy delineates: how to render the invisibility of the encounter of the two sexes without risking its representation, and thus the critique of its representation.

Irigaray comes very close to Gilles Deleuze's philosophy of art in claiming that it is not art's task to give an opinion or make a judgement on the world. Instead, it is to render the aggregations of sensations that our being-in-the-world effects (Deleuze, 2002, p. 31). All art, not only visual art, has this task: to give expression to sensations that are ordinarily inhibited from our modalities of perception. In the non-painterly context of psychotherapy theory and practice, Irigaray liberates painting from the strictures of the aesthetic tradition and links its material resources to the articulation of sexuate subjectivity and culture. In the case of visual perception, Cézanne under-stood well that his job was to paint the sensation because 'sensation is the master of deformations', and when painting links itself to sensation, it 'ceases to be representa-tive and becomes real' (Deleuze, 2002, p. 32, 40). When art forms give expression to sensation, we know that it is neither of the subject nor of the object, but rather *between* subject and object even when the object is an apple. In Irigaray's theorising of painting, we can also hear Deleuze's understandings of the relations of painters to expressions of the invisible and imperceptible forces outside the human being that act on bodies. His account of art as the power of forces affecting living bodies' nervous systems are close to her call to render the sensations of relations between self and other(s) and self and world(s); rendering the sexuate nature of the real that constitutes those relations.

From Irigaray, we know that women need to create the artefacts that would be the symbolic resources to which we can look and with which we can form a feminine imaginary, the lack of which from patriarchy's perspective, has been cited as prevent-ing her accession to culture, and which are necessary for a sexuate culture to be fig-ured. Perhaps more so, women need to heed professional artists' views of art as a form of making that can be extended to wider contexts and applications. In viewing art as a form of *making* where an enduring artefact may (or may not) emerge, but more importantly one where *making* would include making relationships between sexuate subjects that are currently experienced as either formless or contained by forms that are inappropriate to sexuate beings. Irigaray says 'making has seldom been considered as a work carried out *inside* subjectivity' (emphasis added, 2002b, p. 115). By 'inside' here, Irigiaray is talking of women's need to turn inward towards herself, to form a relation of spacing within herself from which she can create forms for herself through her relation(s) with other women and men. The internal movement of self-affection is an artistic formation that Irigaray determined Unica Zürn did not achieve, and is a necessary condition for a sexuate culture to come.

References

Butler, J., Cornell, D., Cheah, P., & Grosz, E. (1998). The future of sexual difference: An interview with Judith Butler and Drucilla Cornell. *Diacritics, 28,* 19–42.

Daley, L. (2012). Luce Irigaray's sexuate economy. *Feminist Theory, 13,* 59–79.

Deleuze, G. (2002). *Francis Bacon. The logic of sensation.* (D. W. Smith, Trans.). Minneapolis: University of Minnesota Press.

Felski, R. (1995). Why feminism doesn't need an aesthetic (and why it can't ignore aesthetics). In P. Z. Brand & C. Korsmeyer (Eds.), *Feminism and tradition in aesthetics* (pp. 431–445). University Park: The Pennsylvania State University Press.

Freud, S. (1961). *Civilisation and its discontents.* (J. Strachey, Trans. & Ed.). New York: Norton Edition.

Grosz, E. (2008). *Chaos, territory, art. A Deleuzian framing of the earth.* New York, NY: Columbia University Press.

Grosz, E. (2012). Irigaray and sexual difference. *Angelaki. Journal of the Theoretical Humanities., 17,* 69–93.

Irigaray, L. (1985a). *Speculum of the other woman.* (G. C. Gill, Trans.). Ithaca, NY: Cornell University Press.

Irigaray, L. (1985b). Is the subject of science sexed? (E. Oberle, Trans.). *Cultural Critique, 1,* 73–88.

Irigaray, L. (1985c). *This sex which is not one.* (C. Porter, Trans.). Ithaca, NY: Cornell University Press.

Irigaray, L. (1993a). *Sexes and genealogies.* (G. C. Gill, Trans.). New York, NY: Columbia University Press.

Irigaray, L. (1993b). *An ethics of sexual difference.* (C. Burke & G. C. Gill, Trans.). Ithaca, NY: Cornell University Press.

Irigaray, L. (1993c). *Je, Tu, Nous. Toward a culture of difference.* (A. Martin, Trans.). New York, NY: Routledge.

Irigaray, L. (1994, May–June). A Natal Lacuna. (M. Whitford, Trans.). *Women's Art Magazine.* No. 58, pp. 11–13.

Irigaray, L. (2002a). *Dialogues.* Special Issue of Paragraph. Edinburgh: Edinburgh University Press.

Irigaray, L. (2002b). *The way of love.* (H. Bostic & S. Pluháček, Trans.). London: Continuum.

Irigaray, L. (2002c). *To speak is never neutral.* (G. Schwab, Trans.). London: Continuum.

Irigaray, L. (2004a). To paint the invisible. (H. Fielding, Trans.). *Continental Philosophy Review, 37,* 389–405.

Irigaray, L. (2004b). To paint the invisible. (H. Fielding, Trans.). *Continental Philosophy Review, 37,* 389–405.

Irigaray, L. (2004c). *Key Writings.* UK: Continuum. London.

Irigaray, L. (2008). *Conversations. Luce Irigaray With Stephen Pluháček, Heidi Bostic, Judith Still, Michael Stone, Andrea Wheeler, Gillian Howie, Margaret R. Miles, Laine M. Harrington, Helen A. Fielding, Elizabeth Grosz, Michael Worton, Brigitte H. Midttun.* London: Continuum.

Irigaray, L. (2013). *In the beginning, she was.* London: Bloomsbury.

Lingis, A. (1968). 'Translator's preface', the visible and the invisible (pp. xl–lvi). Evanston, IL: Northwestern University Press.

Merleau-Ponty, M. (1962). *The phenomenology of perception*. (C. Smith, Trans.). London: Routledge and Kegan Paul.

Merleau-Ponty, M. (1968). *The visible and the invisible*. (A. Lingis, Trans.). Evanston, IL: Northwestern University Press.

Merleau-Ponty, M. (1993a). Cézanne's doubt. In G. A. Johnson (Ed.), *The Merleau-Ponty aesthetics reader* (pp. 59–75). Evanston, IL: Northwestern University Press.

Merleau-Ponty, M. (1993b). Eye and mind. In Galen.A. Johnson (Ed.), *The Merleau-Ponty aesthetics reader* (pp. 121–149). Evanston, IL: Northwestern University Press.

Olkowski, D. E. (2000). The end of phenomenology: Bergson's interval in Irigaray. *Hypatia, 15*, 73–91.

Pollock, G. (1992). Painting, feminism, history. In M. Barrett & A. Phillips (Eds.), *Destablizing theory. contemporary feminist debates* (pp. 138–176). Stanford, CA: Stanford University Press.

Robinson, H. (1995). Irigaray's imaginings. *Women's Art Magazine*, vol. *61*, p. 20.

Schor, M. (1997). *Wet. On painting, feminism and art culture*. Durham, NC: Duke University Press.

Whitford, M. (1994, November–December). Woman With Attitude. *Women's Art Magazine*, vol. *61*, pp. 15–17.

Wittgenstein, L. (n.d). *Remarks on colour*. (G. E. M. Anscombe, Ed., L. L. McAlister, & M. Schättle, Trans.). Oxford: Basil Blackwell.

Ziarek, E. P. (2012). *Feminist aesthetics and the politics of modernism*. New York, NY: Columbia University Press.

All Things Out of Rule

Nuala Gregory

Abstract

This article brings together and compares my own artistic practice of drawing/painting and the eighteenth-century novel Tristram Shandy. *In both cases, there is a free play of lines, textual or graphic, which sets 'all things out of rule'. A whole typology of lines is woven throughout Sterne's text and reappears, alter-inscribed, in the artworks. The article presents an account of these lines: rectilinear, hylomorphic, fractal and nomadic, as well as the line of incision (or the cut). Each is explored as a specific mode of line with differing effects. To follow these lines is to enter a world of material expressivity, to be exposed to an ontology of becoming and change, of flows and transformations, that overturns the traditional ontology of being and stable identity. Sterne's use of wild digression, doodles and graphisms, establishes certain proximity between writing and drawing. Both may be seen as types of 'figured metaphysics' and as ways of bringing something new into the world. The article concludes with some philosophical observations on the strange event of drawing a line, with reference to the work of Heidegger and Deleuze and Guattari.*

Introduction

> A sudden impulse comes across me—drop the curtain, Shandy—I drop it—
> Strike a line here across the paper, Tristram—I strike it—and hey for a new
> chapter! The duce of any other rule have I to govern myself by in this affair
> —and if I had one—as I do all things out of all rule—I would twist it and
> tear it to pieces, and throw it into the fire when I had done—Am I warm?
> I am, and the cause demands it—a pretty story! is a man to follow rules—or
> rules to follow him? (*Tristram Shandy*, IV:10)[1]

Laurence Sterne's (1967) *The Life and Opinions of Tristram Shandy, Gentleman* was published 250 years ago, but has nonetheless been repeatedly cited as a protomodernist, even a postmodernist, novel (Keymer, 2006, p. 14). Its interest, in the present context, is that it functions as a type of 'figured metaphysics' (Mullarkey, 2006, p. 154). That is, it sets out a philosophy—of life, existence or art—through the medium of written and drawn figures and lines. This article will consider two of my own drawn/painted artworks in proximity to *Tristram Shandy* and will use the comparison to tease out a certain relation between writing and drawing. Both are discussed as ways of 'figuring' the world and of bringing something new into the world.

Framed and Unframed Works

To begin with the artworks, the first thing to note is that one (Figure 3) is large-scale and unframed while the other (Figure 1) is smaller and framed behind glass. It may help to focus briefly on the difference introduced by the interposing of the frame between an artwork and its surroundings.

Historically, picture framing evolved from the borders that were placed around ancient tomb paintings (about 3000–4000 years ago) and were later applied to frescos and mosaics.[2] Each of those art forms was fixed into place and its meaning was strongly context-specific. It was not until the Renaissance, when patronage of the arts extended beyond the control of the Church, that paintings became movable objects. And only then did they acquire portable frames designed to complement and enclose the pictures themselves, rather than blend with the surrounding architecture.

Figure 1: *Trikolar*, lithographic monotype, 2010. Photo by Sam Hartnett.

In the modern period, frames increasingly served to define and emphasise the shape of paintings, but also to further isolate them as stand-alone objects. This subtly modified their meaning; the modern tendency is to see a painting as *being* such a discrete *object*, enclosed and delimited by its frame, existing independently in an abstract space that transcends all context.

Typically, the modern frame is a regular polygon with four sides and in most cases, it is rectangular. Given its method of construction, such a frame emerges within a planar space mapped out by four points, or four geometric co-ordinates, which are linked together by lines of connection. Each line, or side of the frame, runs from point to point in a strictly determined fashion. Within this punctual system, it connects together two of the pre-given points in the most efficient possible way, hence the straightness of the lines. They are, as we say, rectilinear.

The narrator of *Tristram Shandy* (VI:40) reminds his readers of the cultural role played by this rectilinear line. He inscribes upon the page 'a line, drawn as straight as I could draw it by a writing-master's ruler', then appends a brief commentary:

> This *right line*,—the path-way for Christians to walk in! say divines—
>
> —The emblem of moral rectitude! says Cicero—
>
> —The *best line!* say cabbage-planters—is the shortest line, says Archimedes, which can be drawn from one given point to another.—

Tristram literally sketches out the relation between recti-*linear* and recti-*tude*: illustrating how righteous conduct follows a path prescribed by a moral code. We orient ourselves in moral space by referring to fixed points of propriety and by plotting a course unerringly between them. This strange geometric vocabulary recalls the logic of Deleuze and Guattari's claim that 'we are made of lines' (Deleuze & Guattari, 2004, p. 215).

In *A Thousand Plateaus*, Deleuze and Guattari deploy the idea of lines to express the creative movement of life itself, the becoming of difference within the world. They describe lines of various sorts. A line may circumscribe a territory, define a trait (of a thing or a person) or intersect with other lines to establish a network of points. These 'molar' or 'segmentary' lines (ibid, p. 215) establish rigidified structures and systems, regulate behaviour and encode the identities of objects, individuals, classes or states. Alternatively, a line may break free from structural containment and volatise all identity in an act of pure escape to the outside. Such a 'line of flight' may happen upon chance connections and map out unprecedented possibilities, before resettling as part of a newly emergent territory or identity; or it may simply dissipate its energy and veer into the void. There is continual interplay between the various lines and their creative and destructive exchanges transform the world by giving birth to the new from within.[3] An important aspect of this theory is that Deleuze and Guattari invert the normal relation between lines and points. In their view, lines precede points and are 'ontologically primary'; they are expressive of movement and becoming, of the real in transformation. Points and positions are derived from the intersection of lines which pass through them; they arrest movement to produce fixed determinations of being such as stable identities and organised systems (Strathausen, 2010, p. 1).

In what follows, Deleuze and Guattari's idea of lines is used as a basis of comparison between writing and drawing, between *Tristram Shandy* and my own artworks.

The Hylomorphic Line

Seen in these terms, the rectilinear lines of a painting's frame go beyond Tristram's moral exhortations to take on an additional, ontological significance. They do this insofar as they connect together to create the *hylomorphic* line: the outline that separates the artwork from the rest of the world and establishes its independence as an object enclosed within its own identity (Zepke, 2005, p. 169).

According to Aristotle, objects come into being as the combination of *hyle* (matter) and *morphe* (form). An active agent, working with a particular model or end in mind, imposes the form of the model upon an inert material. In this hylomorphic ontology, all existing objects are understood as products of 'formed matter'. The intellect is active and does the forming. Matter is inert and passively accepts what is imposed upon it. And that, basically, is how we still tend to think of objects in the world.[4]

This can be seen at work in drawing: the way an object is rendered hylomorphically by tracing its outline. The outline is called a contour line, or a figure. The interior of the drawn object becomes its matter or content. And representation then marks (or re-marks) the passage between the two. To represent is to re-present the matter of an object in an appropriate form through which it is made available both by and for a viewing subject. This is most successfully done when, with a few well-placed lines, the artist captures the essence of something. The Renaissance term *disegno* indicates how drawing is assigned this primary task of capturing essential form. In contrast, painting (*colore*) is assigned the secondary task of colouration, the description of surfaces and textures, the depiction of an object's accidental—that is, non-essential—attributes.

Material Flows and Transformations

The artworks shown here have tended to work counter to this hylomorphic ontology. On reflection, it could be said that these drawings/paintings emerged as acts of departure and difference from the rectilinear (plotted) line—the segmentary line of measurement and control—and the hylomorphic (contour) line that imposes an ideal form upon objects. There was no intention to abolish or go beyond these lines, but rather to play with and subvert their standard meanings, which is why frames and outlines are retained in many of my works. The goal is to reveal something prior to, and ontologically more fundamental than, the world these lines describe—or rather, the world they set up and set in place in such a way that it appears entirely neutral or natural, as a plain fact rather than a constructed representation.

Ingold (2007), anthropologist and author of the book *Lines: A Brief History*, undertakes a similar task when he defines his 'ultimate aim' as:

> to replace [the hylomorphic model] with an ontology that assigns primacy to *processes of formation* as against their final products, and to *flows and*

> *transformations of materials* as against states of matter. Form, to recall Klee's
> words, is death; form-giving is life. (Ingold, 2010, pp. 2–3. Italics added.)

It is these same material flows and transformations that are traced or let loose in my artwork. As in the art of Paul Klee, there is less concern with *representing* the visible than with the act of *making visible*. Reproducing an existing form is less important than the emergence of new 'formless' form. This can be seen quite clearly in the first work.

The coloured lines do not reproduce the forms of recognisable objects. Instead, they give birth to an apparently formless construction made up of neighbouring lines that meet or pass by in flows of indeterminate movement. A thick blue cursive line sweeps up from the bottom centre towards the top right; other blue lines merge with it to create positive and negative spaces. Green and orange lines appear to encroach from above and outside the frame. In contrast to hylomorphism, there appears to be no external agent or finality organising these lines into a closed, representational image. Each line blazes a trail where none previously existed; it forges a path that no map has plotted out; it *becomes* a line through its own immanent displacement across the page.

This type of line is known by various names. Historically, it was called the 'serpentine line' because of its shape, but also to suggest an immanent vitality, a force of self-movement (Bredekamp, 2004, pp. 15–17). It seems to propel itself forward, ignoring all coordinates and pre-plotted paths and threatening to twist free from all fixed identity. Deleuze and Guattari refer to this line variously as the line of flight, the abstract line and, more descriptively, the nomad line which they define as: 'A line of variable direction that describes no contour and delimits no form' (Deleuze & Guattari, 2004, p. 549, 551).

Ontologically, this line does not conform to the idea of inert matter shaped by an external intelligence. Instead, it emerges as a flow of explorative materiality that is formally unprecedented and sensuously particular. That is, it resembles no formal model, and its appearing gives rise to very specific sensations: sensations that motivate or affect us in ways we do not immediately understand. Far from the usual cognitive experience of familiar objects, we enter into a more fundamental encounter—a sensuous or aesthetic encounter—with material forces in expressive movement.

Tristram Shandy (IX:4) includes an example of such a nomad line, a candidate for the most famous doodle in literature. In the midst of a conversation about the freedoms conferred by the state of celibacy, Corporal Trim suddenly brandishes his walking stick:

> Whilst a man is free,—cried the corporal, giving a flourish with his stick
> thus—

Tristram then comments: 'A thousand of my father's most subtle syllogisms could not have said more ...' With these words, Tristram testifies to a surprise encounter with the material expressivity of the gestural line, the flow of stick through air, that, in an instant, surpasses all the demonstrative powers of logical reasoning (Figure 2).

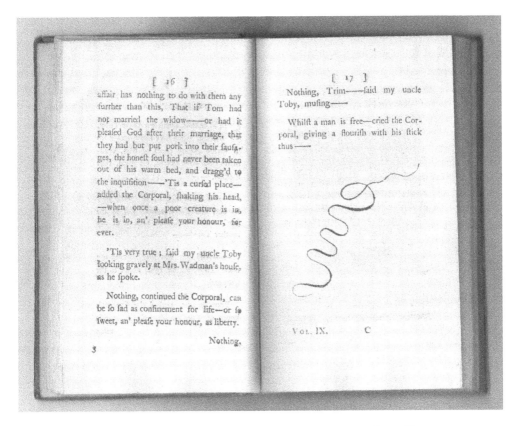

Figure 2: Trim's line from *Tristram Shandy*, 1760, Copyright—The Laurence Sterne Trust.

The inclusion of this nomad line in the midst of the text is of course a visual joke, but a deeply philosophical one. It implies that such a line is more immediate to experience than our language or concepts. In opening up an encounter with expressive materiality (the flourished walking stick, the doodle upon the page), it reminds us that artworks—even novels—are not simply texts to be decoded, logically or semiologically. After all, written words are a type of material inscription, ink on paper, a locutionary form of drawing. Instead, the nomad line provokes an aesthetic sensation that—however contextualised—is not readily amenable to conceptual mediation, but first and foremost, impacts directly on the body, the nervous system, the sensibility. It opens up a realm of sensation and affect, prior to questions of meaning and identity (Deleuze, 2003, p. 37). And it is this material realm, and these questions, that are explored through my own deployment of the nomad line.

Fractal Line

Returning to the work on paper shown in Figure 1, although apparently rectangular in form, it contains no rectilinear lines. Instead, the paper has what is known as a 'deckle edge'. An edge of this type is not cut along a straight line by a guillotine or related device. During the production process, a deckle or framework allows the fibres of pulped paper to congeal freely along the edges, leading to that characteristic 'torn' or 'feathered' look. The process tolerates or releases the expressivity of the materials, granting them the freedom to shift and settle into their own immanent limit.

The deckle edge invites comparison with fractal geometry: an example would be the measurement of a coastline (Mandelbrot, 1967). If a coastline is measured from point to point, say from one headland to another across a beach, this creates a rectilinear and easily measurable line. If a fractal approach is adopted instead, it would require an extremely long piece of thread to be wrapped around every pebble or every grain of sand at the water's edge along the beach, say at low tide. Mandelbrot demonstrates that a fractal line of this sort (a 'limit curve') tends towards infinity in length; its measure depends upon how closely one can wrap into each irregular segment.

For my purposes, deckled paper is a strange kind of readymade. It is deployed to establish a set of non-rectilinear, barely measurable, yet clearly perceptible edges or lines. These, in turn, enclose a mathematically indefinite space within which, or together with which, a further set of lines may be sketched out. The deckle edge acts in tension with the rectilinear frame which is not rejected, but retained as a reminder of those enframing or hylomorphic habits of thought that are being performatively contested from within, by means of the artwork.

In *Tristram Shandy*, something like the fractal line emerges in Tristram's compulsion to delve into the finest details of every particular, digressing at extravagant length rather than pressing on with his narrative. For a 'historiographer', he declares, it is 'morally speaking, impossible … to drive on his history, as a muleteer drives on his mule,—straight forward', and in this matter, Tristram will not confine himself 'to any man's rules that ever lived' (I:4, I:14). An early indication of the narrative's fractal propensities is the tortuous marriage settlement in which clause is embedded within clause, spiralling inwards beyond all reason. Later, Uncle Toby's obsessive modelling of military fortifications acquires the 'complex scaling' of a 'fractilised terrain', a vanishing 'geometry between dimensions' that echoes the structure of the novel as a whole (Freeman, 2002, pp. 154–158).

Modalities of the Cut-out

The second artwork (Figure 3) shows yet another type of line. Despite being made famous by Matisse in the 1940s, the cut-out—or cut-out line—remains relatively undertheorised. To create his *gouaches découpés*, Matisse took a large pair of scissors and set about cutting shapes from coloured papers prepared by his assistants. It is true that his lines tended to be sinuous like the serpentine line; and they produced naturalistic-looking forms that resemble the contour of a body, leaf or flower. And yet, the cut-out could produce effects that were fundamentally different from either.

My own work has deployed the cut-out line in multiple ways. Some paper cut-outs sit raised upon the surface delimiting a positive space, but others are visible as negative outlines only. In the case of *Big Yellow*, a cut-out operation is combined with an operation of expressive materiality.

This large-scale installation began life as 66 sheets of cut paper that were printed in yellow and pinned to a wall. The work was unframed but it retained a

Figure 3: *Big Yellow*, lithographic monotypes and paintings, 2010. Photo by Sam Hartnett.

rectangular-rectilinear form in each of its individual pages and also in the overall ensemble of pages. This outer shape was then subjected to a cut-out operation—the cut-out, in this case, being simply the decision to remove one page at the top right corner, thus destroying the rectangular (geometrically ideal) form of the ensemble. This type of cut-out has yet to be explored *as a line*—a line of decision or of 'the cut'. Etymologically, the verb 'to decide' means to cut off, all of which has clear connections with the cutting and editing work of the art of cinema.

In addition, selected pages from *Big Yellow* were produced using a lithographic technique whose effects inherently challenge the hylomorphic model. As a metaphysics of production, hylomorphism 'invests all productive activity' on the side of form; no agency whatever is attributed to matter (Welchman, 1992, p. 5).[5] Yet, liquid tusche[6] breaks with this understanding by displaying 'auto-induced ... mobile traits of relative formality' (pp. 6–7). In Klee's terms, tusche enacts an immanent process of 'form-giving'. Applied to a lithographic stone, it reveals its distinctive characteristics as it dries out, creating contingent effects of reticulation in the guise of wave-like or web-like patterns. Tusche is also notoriously sensitive to any variation in handling, so that results can be doubly unpredictable: both in particulars of final shape, and in details of surface texture. This stochastic element, or element of chance, was an important dimension of *Big Yellow*. It provides a visible index of the work's guiding aesthetic, which allows for random effects deriving from the immanent qualities of the materials used. The work foregrounds its 'indebtedness' to material flows and transformations through the appearance of contingent patterns of colour and subtly differentiated surface. It thus aligns with Deleuze and Guattari's idea of 'material-forces' which they oppose to the 'matter-form' pairing. Material-forces are less about 'a form capable of imposing properties upon a matter than material traits of expression constituting affects' (Deleuze & Guattari, 2004, p. 407, 451).[7]

Turning again to *Tristram Shandy*, and to the cut-out, the novel contains numerous variations on this operation. The famous black page (I:12) eliminates any possible act of inscription, and two empty chapters (IX:18, 19) confront the reader with a play of narrative absence/material (paper) presence. The 'white' page (VI:38) withholds a written description of the character Widow Wadman; instead, Tristram invites the reader to 'call for pen and ink' to make his own drawing of the widow upon the blank page provided. There is also a 'torn-out' chapter that leaves 'a chasm of ten pages' in the text (IV:25). Tristram adduces contradictory reasons for this extreme act of excision, but refers to a type of line that simply had to be erased. During the repainting of the family's coat of arms, a *bend-sinister* had been mistakenly inserted in place of a *bend-dexter*, thus incorporating a 'vile mark of Illegitimacy' into the Shandy lineage. By inclining in the wrong direction, the line had accrued intolerable meaning. More intolerable still, perhaps, was the unkindest cut of all: five year old Tristram is accidentally circumcised, whilst in mid-urination, by a falling sash window (V:17).

Hylomorphism and the Marbled Page

The typology of lines presented in this article is meant to be indicative rather than comprehensive, but it would be remiss to leave *Tristram Shandy* without a mention of the most enigmatic set of lines of all. This is, of course, the marbled page inserted without explanation at III:36, yet proclaimed by Tristram as 'the motley emblem of my work'. A recent interpretation of this page, devised by Schiff (2000) and advanced by McCaffery (2006), can be fitted nicely within the framework developed here—that is, the page can plausibly be presented as a play on hylomorphism, a cut-out operation and a nomadic 'overcoming' (Figure 4).

The opening scene of the novel goes back before Tristram's birth to the moment of his conception. According to the eighteenth-century theory of the homunculus,[8] the father's sperm contains not only generative force but also the full form of the future human being, in perfect miniature. The homunculus, as Tristram describes him, is a 'little gentleman' in all particulars, transfused *in toto* from father to son and 'escorted' to his worldly destination by 'animal spirits' (I:2). By contrast, the mother's womb is but an inert receptacle: indeed, at one point (IV:29), the novel rehearses the ecclesiastical-legal argument that 'the mother is not of kin to her child'. Welchman (1992, p. 10) nicely derides this idea of uterine nullity, of unformed empty matter, as 'a hylomorphist's wet dream'. Alas, in Tristram's case, his parents' copulation is interrupted (cut) at the critical moment: ejaculation misfires; Tristram's animal spirits are dispersed; his essence is scattered. As a result, his life is predestined to calamity and confusion. In an attempt to overcome this inauspicious beginning, the adult Tristram embarks upon a quest for proper incarnation—he resolves to achieve substantial presence in the world through the act of publishing his 'history'. That history, as it turns out, is a recapitulation as 'sad' and 'disorder'd' as its originary moment: a veritable rhizome of digressions and self-interruptions, recursions and wandering meta-commentary. At intervals, Tristram defends the digressive-progressive 'machinery of [his] work' (I:22). Finally, in a lucid moment, he affirms the deeper truth of the narrative: 'For this is no digression from it, but the thing itself'.[9]

(a)

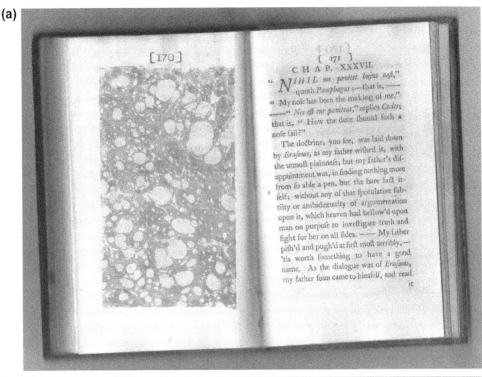

(b)

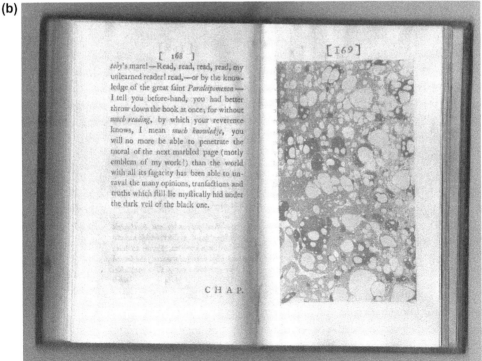

Figure 4: The marbled page from *Tristram Shandy*, 1760, Copyright—The Laurence Sterne Trust.

This is Tristram's moment of nomadic overcoming. He accepts that he is destined to twist free along lines of performative *becoming* that replace hylomorphism's fixed determinations of *being* and identity.

In this wider context, the marbled page can be seen as the original scattering of semen and/or animal spirits;[10] its profusion of lines heralds Tristram's future nomadic becomings. In early editions of the novel, each marbled page was individually hand-produced and inserted into the printed copy (Regan, 2002, pp. 19–21). It stands as the paramount example of Sterne's playfulness with the material form of the novel, also seen in the woodcut lines (VI:40) drawn by Sterne himself, the rearranged and missing chapters, and the countless paratextual and typographical jokes. When feeling his frustrations pile up (VII:30), for example, Tristram writes:

VEXATION

upon

VEXATION

There is an ontological as well as a material dimension to these various jokes. Once again this is epitomised in the figure of the marbled page. In a fascinating article, McCaffery (2006, pp. 66–69) describes a medieval semiotics in which marbling was enlisted to illustrate Christian ideas about incarnation (the penetration of the sensible by the intelligible). Under cover of this religious code, artists of the time began to explore marble's uncanny dynamics of form and formlessness. Painters simulated its capacity to produce 'abstract, variegated, accidental lines', which they used to negate figuration in favour of sensuously particular, aesthetic affects. Given this historical background, McCaffery suggests that *Tristram Shandy's* marbled page and the 'entire formula' of the novel is 'suspended in the ontological paradox of incarnation'. In other words, Sterne's artwork operates at a level more fundamental than, and prior to, any fixed representation (incarnation) of the world. The marbled page that prefig-ures Tristram's life is an emblem of *becoming*: of 'a narrative staging of presence before representation' whose 'strange itinerary' will refuse to settle into a stable body of meanings (p. 67).

What McCaffery has identified is the crucial moment in the background of *Tristram Shandy* with which my own work seeks to make common cause. It is that moment in painting when 'the invisible vacillates and spills into the visual', when sense is given not just through figures, contours and recognisable forms but also, and more funda-mentally, through 'the "cursed part" of paintings, the indexical, non-descriptive, and *dissemblant* part', the part that does not resemble anything (McCaffery, p. 68, quoting Didi-Huberman).[11] This concerns more than the negation of figuration, or an abstract style that forsakes the 'solace of good forms' (Lyotard, 1984, p. 81). It is where paint or line is let loose to run 'all out of rule', where the work engages with contingent materiality, where the artist is caught up in the play of nonsense from which sense must always first emerge. It is this moment that will be taken up in the concluding sections of this essay.

The Primal Scene of Drawing

A useful place to begin is at what Bryson (2003, p. 150) calls the inaugural moment or 'primal scene of drawing'. This occurs whenever a pencil-point is first set upon a white page and begins to be displaced. As the point moves, it deposits a graphite trace that becomes a line. Klee focuses on this inaugural line that is prior to all representational responsibilities: it is no more than *an ongoing presence*, 'an active line on a walk, moving freely without goal'. To illustrate this, Klee draws a series of short lines that twist and curve at will (Klee, 1960, p. 16).

As has been seen, my own painting involves this type of nomad line. But, for now, the argument will be presented via drawing. As the inchoate line emerges, its appearance is accompanied by some strange event in which the 'mechanism' remains unseen —yet which nonetheless transforms the page. No longer just a material effect, the page becomes a surface of inscription and a virtual space of composition. Background and foreground visibly set themselves apart, yet remain conjoined and co-dependent. A strange gap has opened up. But how? An *incision* has been made, unseen, along the path of the drawn line, as the graphite trace advances.

A number of commentators have tried to grasp this uncanny event. For Rosand (2002, p. 2), the pencil 'releases' what Chinese calligraphers call the 'generative' power of the paper, its hidden potential to both *bear* and *bring forth* the image. Bryson (2003, p. 151) also invokes the idea of release. He refers to the whiteness of the page as 'an area without qualities'; but this apparent lack is neither emptiness nor an inertness of matter. Instead, it is a 'reserve'. The specific effect of this reserve (according to Bryson) is to release the act of drawing from the totalising imperative of the art of painting. Conventional 'realistic' painting tends to an aesthetic of finality and closure: the image is given in its final arrested state, as an overall design, in the completed past. In contrast, the reserve of the white page 'sequesters' and 'protects' the inchoate line as it emerges, allowing it to unfold in an ongoing present time, relieved of co-optation into a totalised representation of the world (ibid, p. 151).

If these ideas of reserve and generative potential are combined, they may be thought of as a single material – home, with mom and dad. In the artwork, this material-force—capable of bearing and bringing forth a line whilst also sheltering it—maintains a gap between the self-*presentation* of lines and a binding *representational* image. It can do this for all possible lines, and, by extension, also for colours, textures, words, tones, etc. The idea of such a material-force lies in proximity to what Heidegger calls 'the earth', or simply 'earth'.

Earth and World, Nonsense and Sense

In making this connection, it must be noted that, for Heidegger, earth is neither an entity of any kind nor an independent power. Rather, he sees it as one pole of the dynamic relation between earth and world, which unfolds as a fundamental 'strife' (Heidegger, 1971, p. 49). A world is a total network of practices, relations and significations. A world is the place, and the historical taking place, of meaning.[12] Earth supports that place and that process; in so doing, it makes human dwelling possible. Yet, of all that comes to presence within a world, to overt meaning, earth sustains and shelters a hidden dimension. Earth withdraws into concealment, to a dimension prior to intelligibility and beyond sense.[13] Earth and world are locked in a relation of difference, torn between concealment and unconcealment or 'clearing' (Heidegger, 1971, pp. 53–54).

Whatever presents itself in an artwork (e.g. a line or a colour) divides between a hidden 'earthly' side, and a visible 'worldly' side that partakes in the circulation of meaning. The true artwork activates and stages this immanent difference, bringing it openly into view for the first time. And it does this by means of the *incision* mentioned earlier. That incision may now be understood as the most fundamental cut of all: the *riss* (rend or rift) that separates yet conjoins earth and world as a unity in difference. The *riss* has no visible presence but it inheres in prospective lines of meaning that are sketched out by the artwork and become decisive for its community.[14]

For Heidegger, this is one way in which fundamental change comes about. Indeed, if the artwork is a truly great one, it will help found a new world and a new history.[15] But, to conclude, it will suffice to make more modest claims on behalf of the artwork. The strife of earth and world may, at a certain level, be regarded as a play of sense (the intelligible) and nonsense. Here, nonsense is neither a negation nor an absence, but a name for that excess which remains active within the intelligible even as it withdraws into ultimate impenetrability. It can be seen at work in 'difficult' poetry. Or, take the example of paint. Paint has the potential to be worked up into a meaningful, even decisive, image. View the image too closely, however, and the paint begins to appear either banal or uncanny—an excessive, a-signifying presence. It is given to us to see, but we can make nothing rational of this givenness, this mere 'being there'.

This makes it permissible to say that the written word or painted line is *a play of sense and nonsense,* in which nonsense is not a deficiency to be excluded but is positive and productive. Indeed, this is Deleuze's argument in *The Logic of Sense*. For Deleuze, sense is not just reliable signification or its exchange, nor is it original; sense first has to be produced. What produces it is 'nonsense and its perpetual displacement' (Deleuze, 2004, p. 82). Sense arises as an effect of 'the respective position of elements which are not by themselves signifying'; the flow of formless nonsense 'enacts the donation of sense' (p. 81 and 83). But this event or presentation of sense is reactively reduced by representation to what is uniformly repeatable. The narrator of *Tristram Shandy* is well aware of this conundrum. On the opening page of the novel, no less, Tristram informs us that 'nine parts in ten of a man's sense or his nonsense' depend upon the 'tracks and trains' into which he puts his animal spirits: 'whether right or wrong ... by treading the same steps over and over again, they presently make a road of it'. Since his own animal spirits were dispersed at conception, Tristram's digressions cleave so much closer to nonsense—and reveal so much more of its generative or form-giving power—than the habitual paths walked by others.

In conclusion, it may be claimed that *Tristram Shandy* is an 'Ontologic treasury' (III:19) and masterwork of sense and nonsense. Its wild digressions and excessive comical play *is* the artwork itself. In Deleuze and Guattari's terms, it is an assemblage of multiple lines, albeit a mutant and riotous one. The characters trace out segmentary lines of obsessional behaviour (their various 'hobby horses') which, in Tristram's recounting, erupt into madcap lines of flight that disrupt identity and stable meaning alike. As Tristram's 'history' eludes his grasp and conventions of narrative and novel-istic structure are threatened with collapse, there is an uprising of apparently ungrounded and self-generating new meaning—Tristram's unique brand of nonsensi-cal sense. In Heideggerian terms, Sterne's book performs—or provides a comic rehearsal of—the necessary labour that allows us to trace the emergence of fundamen-tal structures of meaning (world) from the immanent potentialities of material forces (earth) by means of the differential play of inscriptions (art). My own artworks seek to explore broadly similar terrain, attempting to 'figure forth' metaphysical or ontolog-ical ideas in the medium of drawn/painted lines. There is something in the drawn line that leaves a visible trace of its becoming (its coming *into* being) which, if seen correctly, may evoke a feeling for 'being', however understood—as immanent source, as the happening of difference, or as self unfolding creativity.

Notes

1. References to *Tristram Shandy* are given as volume (Roman numeral) and chapter (number).
2. See *A Brief History of The Frame*. Retrieved from http://www.paulmitchell.co.uk/publica tions/history.html.
3. *A Thousand Plateaus* contains a basic typology of lines (see Chapters 1, 8 and 10). The three main types are the molar-segmentary line, the line of flight, and the molecular line (which oscillates between the first two). Within these 'types', there is room for infinite varia-tion depending on context: lines may be described as creative, destructive, connecting, cutting or breaking, cracking etc. The present article applies elements of this typology to specific kinds of line encountered in the context of drawing-writing. On lines generally in Deleuze and Guattari, see Miranda (2013).
4. See Ingold, 2010, p. 2. For a critique of the conceptual pair form-matter, see Heidegger, 1971, p. 27. The hylomorphic line would function as a segmentary line in Deleuze and Guattari's terms.
5. Page numbers for Welchman refer to the online version.
6. Liquid tusche is a greasy, dark wash that is brushed onto a lithographic stone to create specifically 'painterly' effects—the highly variable surface patterns that develop as it dries out. These patterns show up strongly in the final image after the processes of etching, inking and pressing.
7. Deleuze and Guattari (2004) refer to 'a materiality possessing a *nomos*' or internal law (p. 451), and '*a material vitalism* that doubtless exists everywhere but is ordinarily hidden or covered, rendered unrecognisable, dissociated by the hylomorphic model' (p. 454). Italics added.
8. On the homunculus, see Freeman. 'Offering a mock defence of the increasingly discredited homunculus, our narrator [Tristram] seizes upon its impending demise as an opportunity to expose a fault-line in the eighteenth century concept of ontology and identity' (p. 147).
9. Translation of an epigram from Pliny that opens Volume VII: *Non enim excursus hic ejus, sed opus ipsum est*. Earlier Tristram writes: 'Digressions, incontestably, are the sunshine; — they are the life, the soul of reading' (I:22).
10. McCaffery (pp. 65–66) quotes Schiff: 'In the context of the narrative, it is obvious that this image represents Walter Shandy's ejaculation ... The colours of the original marbled page can all be found in the body, and white and yellow pigments are splattered in the top layer'.

11. Didi-Huberman (1995, p. 45) traces the concept of *dissemblance* back to Plato. For medieval theology, God was *dissemblant* in that nothing resembles him; he is the formless ground of all form (p. 52).
12. Heidegger defines world as a 'relational totality' of 'significance' (1962, p. 120), and as an 'open relational context' for a 'historical people' (1971, p. 42).
13. Young (2002, p. 9) describes world (in Heidegger) as the *intelligible* as opposed to the *unintelligibility* of earth.
14. Heidegger (1971, p. 63) plays on the verbs *reissen* (to break open, rend) and *ziehen* (to pull, draw) to suggest that the artwork sets up a 'basic design' and 'outline sketch' of inaugural meaning. On the *riss*, see Chapter 4 of Fynsk (1993), and also McGuirk (2011).
15. Ibid, p. 77: 'Whenever art happens—that is, whenever there is a beginning—a thrust enters history, history either begins or starts over again'.

References

Bredekamp, H. (2004). Frank Gehry and the art of drawing. In M. Rappolt & R. Violette (Eds.), *Gehry draws* (pp. 11–28). Cambridge, MA: MIT Press.

Bryson, N. (2003). A walk for a walk's sake. In C. De Zegher (Ed.), *The stage of drawing: Gesture and act. Selected from the Tate collection* (pp. 149–158). New York, NY: Tate Publishing and The Drawing Center.

de Miranda, L. (2013). Is a new life possible? Deleuze and the lines. *Deleuze Studies, 7,* 106–152.

Deleuze, G. (2003). *Francis Bacon: The logic of sensation.* New York, NY: Continuum.

Deleuze, G. (2004). *The logic of sense.* London: Continuum.

Deleuze, G., & Guattari, F. (2004). *A thousand plateaus: Capitalism and schizophrenia.* New York, NY: Continuum.

Didi-Huberman, G. (1995). *Fra Angelico: Dissemblance and figuration.* Chicago, IL: Chicago University Press.

Freeman, J. (2002). Delight in the (dis)order of things: Tristram Shandy and the dynamics of genre. *Studies in the Novel, 34,* 141–161.

Fynsk, C. (1993). *Heidegger.* Thought and historicity: Cornell University Press.

Heidegger, M. (1962). *Being and time.* (J. Macquarrie & E. Robinson, Trans.). Oxford: Basil Blackwell.

Heidegger, M. (1971). *Poetry, Language, thought.* New York, NY: Harper & Row.

Ingold, T. (2007). *Lines: A brief history.* New York, NY: Routledge.

Ingold, T. (2010). *Bringing things to life: Creative entanglements in a world of materials.* NCRM Working paper #15, Realities/The Morgan Centre, University of Manchester. Unpublished paper. Retrieved from http://www.socialsciences.manchester.ac.uk/morgancentre/realities/wps/

Keymer, T. (Ed.). (2006). *Laurence Sterne's Tristram Shandy: A casebook.* Oxford: Oxford University Press.

Klee, P. (1960). *Pedagogical sketchbook.* New York, NY: Praeger Publishers.

Lyotard, J.-F. (1984). *The postmodern condition: A report on knowledge.* Minneapolis, MN: University of Minnesota Press.

Mandelbrot, B. B. (1967). How long is the coast of Britain? Statistical self-similarity and fractional dimension. *Science, New Series, 156,* 636–638.

McCaffery, S. (2006). *A chapter of accidents. Public, 33*: Errata, 64–73. Retrieved from http://pi.library.yorku.ca/ojs/index.php/public/article/viewFile/30087/27648

McGuirk, T. (2011). The 'rift-design' conundrum: Drawing as form-giving and knowing. *ACCESS: Critical Perspectives on Communication, Cultural & Policy Studies, 30,* 45–56.

Mullarkey, J. (2006). *Post-continental philosophy: An outline.* London: Continuum.

Regan, S. (2002). Print culture in transition; Tristram Shandy, the reviewers and the consumable text. *Eighteenth-Century Fiction, 14*. Retrieved from http://digitalcommons.mcmaster.ca/ecf/vol14/iss3/18

Rosand, D. (2002). *Drawing acts: Studies in graphic expression and representation*. Cambridge: Cambridge University Press.

Schiff, K. (2000). Topics in the history of artists' books: Tristram Shandy's original marbled page. *The Journal of Artists' Books, 14*, 6–11.

Sterne, L. (1967). *The life and opinions of Tristram Shandy, gentleman*. London: Penguin Books. (Originally published in nine volumes 1759–1767.)

Strathausen, C. (2010). Epistemological reflections on minor points in Deleuze. *Theory & Event, 13*. Retrieved from Project MUSE database.

Welchman, A. (1992). On the matter of chaos. In J. Broadhurst-Dixon (Ed.), *Deleuze and the transcendental unconscious*, special edition of *Pli: Warwick Journal of Philosophy*. Vol. 4 (pp. 137–157). Retrieved from http://www.academia.edu/1187174/On_the_matter_of_chaos

Young, J. (2002). *Heidegger's later philosophy*. Cambridge: Cambridge University Press.

Zepke, S. (2005). *Art as abstract machine: Ontology and aesthetics in Deleuze and Guattari*. New York, NY: Routledge.

Activating Built Pedagogy: A genealogical exploration of educational space at the University of Auckland Epsom Campus and Business School

Kirsten Locke

Abstract

Inspired by a new teaching initiative that involved a redesign of conventional classroom spaces at the University of Auckland's Epsom Campus, this article considers the relationship between architecture, the built environment and education. It characterises the teaching space of the Epsom Campus as the embodiment of educational policy following its inception in the early 1970s. Heralded as a modernist work of architecture juxtaposing material and textural combinations, the Epsom Campus emerged as a metaphorical vanguard of teaching pedagogy that stood as a symbol of a more progressive and culturally inclusive style of education. With consideration for a different kind of architectural space and pedagogy at the city-based business school, the article extends an understanding of spatiality and learning, and argues the structural architectonics of the teaching space and the built environment confer their own pedagogical value. By drawing on the critical stance of Nietzsche's genealogical methodology for reading history, strands of historical discourse and 'vibrant materialities' are considered so that the 'built pedagogy' of both contexts can be activated and explored.

Introduction

Classroom structures and the physicality of teaching spaces are not benign. The purpose of this article is to illustrate the way buildings convey their own messages, solidified and materialised through physical walls and demarcated spaces, about the purposes of education. This article focuses on these spatial sites of pedagogy as the ideological terrain on which competing ideas are played out and educational purpose made manifest. Particular attention is given to the idea that this spatial or *spatialized* site of pedagogy is the interrelation between the embodied actions of what we do as teachers, and the physical spaces *where* we do it. Embodiment in this context is considered 'a generative site of epistemological understanding' (Senior & Dixon, 2009,

p. 21), where bodies, spaces, matter and immateriality intersect in education and have the potential to create new meanings. This interrelational dimension draws on a strain of architectural thought that conceives of architecture and space as not simply consisting of a dualism between designed object and social use, but instead as active constituents of social relations that intersect in dynamic and fluid ways. With reference to the philosopher Henri Lefebvre, Borden (2000) describes this architectural reconceptualization as a 'space of flows—not as an object in space, but as the product of, and interrelation between, things, spaces, individuals and ideas' (p. 224). As a socially constructed site of interrelations, the embodiment of teaching and learning is defined and redefined within these borders and, in turn, demarcates the borders of the educational space.

This article was written in response to the introduction of interactive large class teaching at the Faculty of Education, University of Auckland, New Zealand in 2012. This new teaching initiative required a restructuring of classrooms to accommodate groups of approximately 60 students in one space. A pressing problem was to make classes physically larger, and this usually involved knocking down a wall between two standard-sized classrooms to create larger spaces. The enlarged room then underwent a substantial technological refit with large screens positioned at various places on the classroom walls, usually with a main screen and projector at the front of the room. Instead of desks in rows or groups, the furniture was fitted with hexagonal tables that were formed by separate modular desks. Ipads were allocated to numbers of students to ensure interactivity, and lecturers' teaching in these rooms underwent a series of training programmes to help integrate the different technological interfaces into their teaching practice. While not universally rolled out in all Initial Teacher Education courses, many students and lecturers have now experienced the initiative.

This new teaching initiative ignited my curiosity. I was initially interested to find out that the Business School at the University of Auckland had also implemented these changes to the teaching delivery of the heavily prescribed first-year paper that fed into various commerce degree pathways. However, what interested me particularly were the different intended outcomes between the two initiatives, and then as I thought about this more, what the physical shifts of classroom spaces that both sites had to undertake meant in the context of education. The Business School had implemented these changes for reasons that would have been specific to the context of the discipline being taught, and the physical site where these teachers and students learnt this knowledge. The interactive large classes at the Faculty of Education would necessarily have different needs and, certainly, a different teaching context and purpose. The Business School would be readying its students for the world of commerce. The Faculty of Education, predominantly, serves the purpose of preparing future teachers. To a certain extent, the space of teaching at the faculty is where the theoretical and practical 'organs' of pedagogical methods, approaches and theories of learning and teaching are laid bare. While both the Business School and the Faculty of Education deal with engaging students with new technologies and teaching methods for the purpose of teaching and generating knowledge, the aims of the schools are necessarily different: at the Faculty of Education, the purpose is to teach students about, and how, to teach—an altogether different reason for being from that of the Business School.

There were other factors that fed my curiosity and growing interest in these changes. The Faculty of Education is located in the inner-city suburb of Auckland in Mount Eden, approximately four and a half kilometres away from the Business School that is located in the city centre where the University of Auckland has its main campus. This geographical distance is mirrored in the different ages and architectural styles of the buildings. The group of buildings at the Epsom Campus, as it stands today, were built between 1973 and 1978 (with further modifications that continued at various intervals and still continues to this day), while the Business School was built to great fanfare in 2007 and as yet has not undergone any significant reconstruction. The Epsom Campus buildings are a material and discursive outcome of the 1970s. In 2004, the Campus (which was then Auckland College of Education) amalgamated with the University of Auckland. The Business School, housed in the Owen G Glenn Building at the University of Auckland city campus, is a product of 2007, steeped in a confidence in the knowledge economy and the university's aim to claim a leading position in the 'knowledge wave'. Both the Business School and Epsom Campus exist in the present neoliberal and globalised world, and in both cases, the introduction of large class teaching needs to be read in this context. In order to do this, and to build on the notion of interrelationality between spaces, embodiment and educational discourses, I utilise the idea of *built pedagogy* that is infused within the form of the buildings, where educational intent is concretised into solid mass that physically shapes and defines the spaces and borders of the educational endeavour. The density of the solid block forms of the Epsom Campus and the fluid, floating, glassed transparency of the Owen G Glenn Building 'speak' to us about pedagogy as the style and intent of what we do as teachers at the university; they activate a version of their own built pedagogy that we embody and are constituted by. This article maintains these educational spaces impact on the social; they not only 'express social relationships but also react upon them' (Rendell, 2006, p. 17), thus constituting a particular kind of pedagogy that has particular aims.

To complement the discussion, I use a genealogical perspective to explore the Epsom Campus and the Owen G Glenn Building that utilises the historic notions of descent and emergence to reveal what Foucault (1979), via Nietzsche, refers to as the 'histories of the present'. To do this, I focus on the different histories that animate the present twilight of the perceived usefulness of the Epsom Campus as the home of the Faculty of Education, and the histories of the present that animate the current vitality of the Business School. The identified histories illustrate the rich interplay between buildings and people, space and mass, physical and spiritual environment, and educational policy and intent. While there are examples of historical and artistic explorations of university sites (see for instance Edquist & Grierson, 2008), this discussion is concerned with various archived narrative strands of a genealogical analysis that are woven into the history of the Epsom Campus and the Owen G Glenn Building, constituting what Bennett calls the vibrant matter of our lived environment (Bennett, 2010). The genealogy I present draws on the critical stance of Nietzsche's methodological approach to history that allows the existence of vibrant materialities and matter in a critical history of the built pedagogy to emerge. It is to a closer examination of Nietzsche's genealogy that I now turn.

Doubling the 'Built': Place/Time—Pedagogy/Architecture

> Genealogy is gray, meticulous, and patiently documentary. It operates on a field of entangled and confused parchments, on documents that have been scratched over and recopied many times. (Foucault, 1991, p. 76)

Foucault's opening statement to his essay 'Nietzsche, Genealogy, History' (Foucault, 1991) evocatively depicts the complex webbing of genealogical discourse. This one statement contains within it the active, temporal dimension to genealogical analysis with its reference to 'scratching over', rewriting and 're'-copying the threads of discourse that make up the conventional narratives of history so that a standard truth in the past may be questioned, rewritten and put to the test. For Foucault, 'the past actively exists in the present', as it 'continues to secretly animate' life in its contemporaneous, temporal and affective states (1991, p. 81). While Foucault famously utilises this approach as a guiding methodology throughout much of his mid-to-late thinking, the inspiration for looking at history differently so as to provide greater insight into the present, first emerges from Nietzsche. In the essay entitled 'On the uses and disadvantages of history for life' in the *Untimely Meditations* (1983), Nietzsche, writing in 1874, explores the way historical knowledge can enhance the present, but only if we can resist the urge to reify the past so that the present avoids stultification. Foucault picks up on Nietzsche's questioning of the way history is accessed and utilised for its own sake, as was certainly Nietzsche's argument in the time and place of his writing context in nineteenth century Germany. Nietzsche argued that history can only have a useful and therefore beneficial affect when it is brought in to the present 'for the purposes of life' as a critical history of the present (1983, p. 64).

Nietzsche's meaning of the 'purposes of life' is where genealogy comes to the fore as an alternative lens with which to view and treat history, and where my approach to looking at the historical past becomes relevant. For Nietzsche, history is split into three versions: monumental, antiquarian and critical. While monumental and antiquarian views of history deal with models for living and existing in the world that draw on past events, and models of cultures which justify the existence of *man* as a constantly developing and improving creature of reason, critical history questions all absolutes and truths. For Nietzsche, to live fully in the present required a person to 'employ the strength to break up and dissolve a part of the past: he does this by bringing it before the tribunal, scrupulously examining it and finally condemning it' (Nietzsche, 1983, p. 76). To be critical of the past, in this context, is to be productively active in the present with an aim to move beyond and away from one's own culture and history, to a vital and rich engagement with the conditions of existence in order to activate these conditions in a 'present-ness' of the present. Being critical, in Nietzsche's view, requires a fine balance between knowing the past in a historical sense, yet having the facility to look beyond the past by living in the present in an *un*historical way. By unhistorical, Nietzsche is intimating a necessary 'ability to forget'. He goes on to explain, 'the unhistorical and the historical are necessary in equal measure for the health of an individual, of a people and of a culture' (1983, p. 63).

It is this genealogical view of history that inspired my analysis of the Epsom Campus in the context of newer institutional buildings such as the Owen G Glenn

Building, and the ways they act on, create and maintain educational imperatives that are products of their time and place in New Zealand's educational history. Foucault's use of genealogy and architecture is most famously encapsulated in the disciplining spatiality of the panopticon, an all-seeing, behaviour-regulating mechanism of disciplinary power (Foucault, 1979). However, it is Nietzsche's approach to the telling of history more critically, and the importance of the temporal *unhistoricisity* and spontaneity of the present, that can also be helpful when applied alongside a spatial history of educational discourse. The genealogy in the following sections examines some historical evidence of the Epsom Campus and considers this alongside the emergence of the Owen G Glenn Building. The affective unhistorical dimension from Nietzsche is then woven into a discussion of vibrant matter and vital pedagogies.

Place/Time: Epsom Campus

Thanks to a large cohort of baby boomers entering higher education, it became increasingly apparent in the late 1960s that the existing brick building at the Auckland Teachers College in the inner-city Auckland suburb of Mt Eden was simply not big enough for the post-war baby boomers it needed to accommodate (Shaw, 2006). In 1967, the prominent Auckland architectural firm of Thorpe, Cutter, Pickmere and Douglas was approached, and in 1973, the first architectural plans were finalised. The intention was to incorporate both the primary and secondary teacher training colleges, previously housed separately in different buildings, on one unified site. A senior architect on the project, Jack Manning, described the brief as follows:

> The decision was made to turn Auckland Teachers' College, which was a primary teaching college, into both a secondary and primary teaching college one on the same site. So there was a new primary building, a new secondary building, a teaching building, a gymnasium for each, a library to be shared between the two and common rooms for the students. I was the architect in charge of the project. David Mitchell had come to work at the firm and he was another senior architect on it, and there were a whole lot of graduates straight out of architecture school, people like Peter Sargisson, Neil Simmons and Peter Hill. (Manning, 2011)

The proposed replacement of the imposing brick building would need to take into consideration the population of the student body, the different forms of teaching qualification and the different functions of the teaching space. From the outset, the redevelopment of the site stood for the more progressive and inclusive approach to education for which the college positioned itself as a major leader. The buildings that materialised emerged as a metaphorical vanguard of teaching pedagogy that stood as a symbol for this newer style of education. Epsom Campus was shaping to be a radical redevelopment, from an imposing brick structure reminiscent of an austere style of education that mirrored very strongly the grammar school model, to one of progress, growth, innovation and the 'new' New Zealand of political activism, hard-won cultural independence and identity, and an education system that would be ready to tackle growing societal inequalities.

The redesigned site proposed housing the two colleges through the unifying thread of a meandering pathway that traversed the entire campus. Students would be able to walk freely into any space, up or down, in any direction, regardless of what they were studying. The pohutakawa and the many old trees that had been planted on the site were an important structural element to take into consideration. The genealogy of the trees, such an important contemporary testimony to the history of the campus, were first planted by the Grierson family whose homestead 'Longmead' occupied a portion of the land between 1908 and 1921 (Gray, 2011), and then by the first two decades of students beginning the first year the site opened as a college in 1926 (Trussell, 1981). Also of importance was the birdlife, the structural configurations of the volcanic slopes that provided the contours of the campus, and the surrounding suburban setting. Not only would the redesign of the campus infuse the progressive and innovative elements of education, but the designers themselves wanted to craft something different and cutting edge. The primary training section and the secondary training section each had different designers, accounting for the quite different stylistic characteristics between buildings. One of the other senior architects was David Mitchell. In the New Zealand architectural programme, 'The Elegant Shed' Mitchell discusses with Jack Manning the point of difference of the Epsom designs to the brutal concrete and glass boxes that were taking the cities of New Zealand by storm.

> Well at that time, I think every architect working on an office block had the same attitude. They were all pretty much in love with glass boxes. It was an attitude that had started with Lever House and Seagram House in New York and was repeated thousands of times after that, getting gradually worse as time went on … I don't know whether it was a conscious reaction against that …we all had an attitude that was quite different. The main materials are fibrolite, which has got a spray coating on them and inside that there are just acres and acres of good old Kiwi timber framing. So the materials are basically very simple and very economical. I suppose you'd say this is probably New Zealand's first large, high-tech building and the use of steel and colour and fairly light, elegant materials was all part of the language architects were using at that time. (Manning in Mitchell, 1984)

Construction took place between 1973 and 1978, with the final dismantling of the old brick building in 1976 (Shaw, 2006, p. 170). Teaching continued throughout the construction, and there was a palpable feeling of an emerging brave new world in education, an excitement and sense of anticipation that seemed to run through the buildings themselves as their curved turrets and glassed enclosures started to take form. The political landscape, like that of the campus, was also changing during the 1970s, and the significance of the redeveloped campus at this time was heightened as it became a symbol of standing strong in defiance to wider societal challenges. Jack Manning commented on this liveliness:

> It was a really lively team and the buildings that resulted from it were quite striking. They were fairly simply built. There was a fair amount of raw concrete and we used a lot of cement panels as cladding, pre-coated with

polyurethane. This was often in dazzling whites and primary colours. There were some quite startling things about the buildings that were really quite vibrant and vital. (Manning, 2011)

The campus is not only vital, as Jack Manning describes, but also playful and whimsical in places. The classroom 'prefab' (that most New Zealand of school architectural icons), serves as a motif that the designers clearly riff on in the shapes of the teaching spaces and larger building structures. This is a campus that feels very much like the schools it was, and is, preparing its student population. There are many entry points to the campus; the porous boundaries of the site offer a clever counterpoint to the dense weightiness of some of the blocked shapes. The metaphor is that learning is contained within these blocks, but the space of education itself is pliable and changeable. The softness of the many curves complement and complicate the strong, mechanistic lines of the buildings, and the glassed stairwells and exposed pipes give a cheeky wink to the 'nuts and bolts' of the teaching profession. Couched in the humour, of course, is the notion that the exposure of the inner workings of the building to the outside elements, signals a darker hint of the exposed nature of the teaching profession to notions of surveillance and transparency. Education, if the buildings we work in are anything to go by, in its essence, is not a straightforward journey. It meanders, it can be a little shambolic, there are many different perspectives on how we do things, and not everything is tied to a perfect and predictable outcome. Implicit within this exploration is the related notion that the translation between the architectural idea and architectural object is never a simple straight line, but that many affects, threads of discourse and conceptual meanings complicate and constitute the lived, embodied spaces that emerge (Ingraham, 1998). Epsom campus is in some important way the tangible manifestation of a built pedagogy that draws on the genealogy of many different dimensions such as trees, birds and volcanic ground that gives specificity to the local environment in which this built pedagogy is situated.

Pedagogy/Architecture: Owen G Glenn Building

The Owen G Glenn Building has its own version of built pedagogy with educational aims that converge and diverge with those of the Faculty of Education. Both educational spaces aim to engage learners and use technology in new large interactive teaching spaces, yet their differences when applying a Nietzschean genealogical lens can be identified beyond these similarities. The Owen G Glenn Building is a leaner, meaner beast of space and form transplanted directly from other renowned international business schools. This is no locally derived or sourced building in ideology or intent. Sturm and Turner (2011) trace the architectural lineage of the Owen G Glenn Building to the Hult International Business School, the Simmons School of Management and the Massachusetts Institute of Technology Sloan School of Management. They draw on the New Zealand Herald article that announced this triumphant addition to the University of Auckland in 2007 in the following:

> The building cuts and thrusts. Its façade, in bands of shiny glass and aluminium, curves as a bay out to jutting headlands. Glass blades sweep

past the building's ends, slicing the air. It means business. (cited in Sturm & Turner, 2011, p. 28)

Sturm and Turner offer an alternative response to the building, describing the style as 'transcendental university architecture', a form of 'neoliberal gothic where, like old Gothic a transcendental architecture comprised of space, light, line and geometry' (p. 12) reaches not for the God in the heavens, but boldly outwards. This is the temple to transcendental capitalism that Sturm and Turner identify as being the third stream to the purpose of the university that was added in to the strategic direction of the University of Auckland. This third stream, apart from the aims of teaching and research at the university, includes business partnerships and alliances. The Owen G Glenn Building is a template that is 'vectoral, its out-reaching arcs tracing the flight lines of transcendental capital that punctuate and striate, and so redistribute, local space' (ibid.). The transparency of the glass façade in the Owen G Glenn Building signals no building and empty space, or at least space 'filled' with nothing that, following Casey (1997), seems to present no sense of its unique *place* when contrasted with the humour and whimsy of the Epsom Campus.

The transparency of the glass gives the Owen G Glenn Building the appearance and feeling of other big, utilitarian structures such as an airport or conference centre. This is an indoor–outdoor flow taken to the extreme. Unlike the solid forms of the Epsom Campus, the Owen G Glenn Building suggests a free-floating timelessness, unburdened by historical and individual narratives. Enclosed under the fluid glass are the customers, travelling through the building to their destinations beyond the enclosure, using the facilities, refuelling on fast knowledge on their ways. Like the free-flowing transcendental capital it symbolises, the students move freely only on the first and second floors, while the floors above are left free to let intellectual capital flow and academic business happen.

But what of the built pedagogy in the Owen G Glenn Building? This space encourages clean transmission of information, easily tested nuggets of economic gold that turn into data quicksilver able to travel in an instant to the waiting receptacle of the university central nervous system of Cecil, the University of Auckland online interface that deals with course information, timetables and some forms of assessment. Like the instant flows of capital the Business School covets, information in this context must flow unaided and without obstacles. Drawing on Nietzsche, the built pedagogy at play as a history of the present in this building is animated by transcendental neoliberalism within which abstract forms of space, capital and commerce resonate. Like the Epsom Campus, the Owen G Glenn Building is currently produced through neoliberal imperatives, and in the case of the Business School, it is situated in the Central Business District of Auckland where the focus can be closely aligned to the discourses and flows of commerce that constitute the business at the heart of the city. This focus on commerce is one of the interesting divergences between the two institutional sites, where as at Epsom Campus, a more 'pastoral' dimension is evoked in which the relational aspects of education can flourish.

Vibrant Materialities as Built Pedagogy: Bringing Histories to Life

The built pedagogy of Epsom Campus also includes the negative space, that is, the space that outlines the silhouette of the buildings and wider campus that forms the shape of the campus as a whole. It is here that Bennett's notion of vibrant matter can be linked to narrative threads that can be incorporated into an activation of the built pedagogy of the campus. It is also at this point that a genealogical lens is further applied to Bennett's application of a 'vital materiality' that follows Nietzsche's dictum of a critical history that *animates* the present. The intention of exploring Bennett's vibrant matter through the built environment is, following Nietzsche, to bring these historical threads to life for the purposes of enriching our present understandings of the built pedagogy of the Epsom Campus. Bennett defines vibrant matter as organic and inorganic matter that, taking inspiration from the philosopher Spinoza, is 'not inert matter, but lively intensities, vibrant materialities' (2010, p. viii). Bennett looks at the way Spinoza incorporated this sense of vibrant materiality of things into a drive within matter to seek alliances with other inorganic and organic forms to enhance vitality. Of importance to my Nietzschean application of vibrant matter, is the way Bennett deconstructs the primacy of the subject, over things, environment and inorganic matter. Instead for Bennett, *things* as objects and matter have as much 'agentic capacity' (2010, p. 9) as thinking beings, thus allowing the Epsom Campus and its 'built' environment a status other than merely passive and *un*-affective. It is at this point I am placing the Epsom Campus within a gravitational pull where suddenly the borders of its space become significant and alive, where things and histories become part of the vitality of the campus as a whole.

At the edge of the expansive playing field of the Epsom Campus is the first form of vibrant matter I identify as the normal school that borders the campus, Auckland Normal Intermediate. The expansive green lushness of the fields belies what was once part of a rough lava-field from the nearby volcano of Maungawhau, also known as Mt Eden, when the original building of the Campus was first populated with students (Shaw, 2006, p. 73). The grounds that surrounded the original brick building were covered in gorse and rocks that had to be levelled, and it would take another couple of years before the playing fields that join the two sites together were fit for purpose. From its inception in 1923, Epsom Campus was to include a purpose-built normal school, and by 1928 Mount Eden Normal School was built 'comprising eight classrooms and a large criticism room' (Shaw, 2006, p. 81). It is not by accident that the space of teacher training is next to a school. There are historic and pragmatic reasons for this that are significant to any ideas about pedagogy as something that must be learnt, that requires technical and theoretical knowledge, that has a distinct body of knowledge, and that contributes to the notion of teaching as a profession (Openshaw & Ball, 2006). Like the radical change of landscape from rocky, gorse-covered, unlevelled land to flat, grassed expanse, the close vicinity of a school to the Epsom Campus and the connecting land that joins it, serves as a constant reminder of the 'hewn' dimension to the craft of teaching as something that has the power to transform.

Also on the edges of the Epsom Campus stand the memorial gates dedicated to the Auckland teachers who fought and died in the First World War. Officially opened in

1932, the gates stood at the entrance to the original brick building providing a sense of grandeur and patriotic fervour to the campus. Made from Portland stone left over from the Auckland War Memorial Museum, the gates were crafted by unemployed stonemasons during the Depression and were 'symbolically linked' to the campus with the continuing programme of planting native New Zealand trees such as manuka, kauri and pohutakawa (Shaw, 2006, p. 87). A further genealogical link is that the architectural firm of Grierson, Aimer and Draffin designed the Auckland War Memorial Museum. One of the architects was Hugh Grierson who lived as part of the Grierson family on the Epsom Campus site at Longmead, and the Portland stone that was left over from the War Memorial Museum provides another genealogical thread that animates the present history of this site. While Hugh Grierson survived Passchendaele, his brother Walter was killed in the First World War (Vail, 2011) and the stone that links these two memorial sites is imbued with individual loss even as it testifies to public trauma. Belich (2001) described the First World War as a mincing machine, where New Zealanders were sent to fight, even when there was knowledge of the futility of the situation, and were sentenced to death with no control over how this would happen. Belich also identifies the sustained ideological programme that emerged after the First World War that celebrated heroism and loyalty, of which education took a leading role. Now aged with moss and darkened with time and rust, the memorial gates no longer stand starkly as the main entrance of Epsom campus, and instead crouch into the shade provided by the grown trees as a side entrance that services the normal school. As an example of vibrant matter, these gates are an important narrative thread that symbolise the way education is always situated within a wider social, political and ideological fabric.

Another example of vibrant matter is a single tree that stands outside what is now the administrative block of the campus. In a small brown paper envelope in the Sylvia Ashton Warner Library archives, there is a photo that is slightly blurred and yellowed, of people planting a small tree. There is no date on the photo and no caption describing what this tree planting ceremony was in aid of. Yet that tree now stands tall and strong, like many other trees that provide so much of the built environment of the campus. This little tree was planted, and somehow, has endured. There is no plaque, just a yellowed photograph stored in the archives testifying to its significance. This piece of anonymous history, of one tree that was planted in a ceremony that bears no mark of time other than to show the 'new' buildings of the redevelopment is what acts as a vital materiality. As an example of placing history to the uses and advantage of life, this article is somehow testifying to this one tree's enduring significance. In this context, the tree signals growth, change and affect in the life of the present.

Not far from the tree is the campus marae, named 'Tutahi Tonu Wharenui'. It seems a glaring omission, looking back from today's vantage point, that a marae was not part of the original plans of the redevelopment but this in itself also says something interesting about education in New Zealand at one particular point in time. In the decade of the 1970s when the campus was redeveloped, a growing international discourse of decolonisation, marked by a local strengthening and momentum of Maori activism and identity, was making its appearance felt. By the time of the opening of Tutahi Tonu where 1500 people took part in the opening ceremony in 1983, the

Treaty of Waitangi negotiations were first beginning to be linked to educational policy aims. Since then, Tutahi Tonu now stands as a symbol of diversity and inclusivity that is part of the built pedagogy of this campus. The word marae refers to 'space' and the wharenui is the building. The wharenui at the Epsom Campus has a plaque that talks of enduring presence, continuity, standing steadfast in this place: 'We stand day and night, we stand as one'. According to a local legend, Māori tupuna brought some earth with them from their ancestral homeland Hawaiki and buried a handful of that earth into the volcanic crater on this site. Tutahi Tonu is the built manifestation that signifies *building* Maori identity and culture into prominence in New Zealand's educational discourse, and bears testimony through local legend and myth, to the spiritual dimension and connections of teaching and learning that help deconstruct colonised space.

Concluding Comments

This article took as its inspiration the implementation of a new teaching initiative and the significant shifts this initiative precipitated in physical classroom borders and spaces at the Faculty of Education, University of Auckland. My intention has been to link an exploration of these material shifts with a genealogical analysis of affective spatialities that constitute and activate what I have termed the built pedagogy of the Epsom Campus and Owen G Glenn Building. Since its inception, the large class teaching spaces have provided an array of challenges and opportunities for innovative pedagogical approaches at the Faculty of Education. With a growing international literature on the effectiveness of these spaces (see for instance Brooks, 2012; Salter, Thomson, Fox, & Lam, 2013), and an increasingly receptive audience in the university academic sphere to teaching innovation, the initiative looks set to develop further both internationally and locally. However, my intention has been to broaden an exploration from the changing materialities of classroom spaces to the wider built environment, and to explore this built environment as part of a more expansive conversation on the metaphorical, symbolic and affective spatialities of learning and teaching. Presented as a genealogy of spatial and affective histories, I have drawn attention to the critical dimensions of the physical and historical shifts that have taken place between two educational sites at the University of Auckland in order to explore the built pedagogy that animates both teaching contexts. Finally, this article has offered an alternative lens with which to view these histories, following Nietzsche, for the advantage of *educational* life.

References

Belich, J. (2001). *Paradise reforged: A history of the New Zealanders from the 1880s to the year 2000*. London: Penguin Books.

Bennett, J. (2010). *Vibrant matter: A political ecology of things*. Durham, NC: Duke University Press.

Borden, I. (2000). Thick edge: Architectural boundaries in the postmodern metropolis. In I. Borden & J. Rendell (Eds.), *Intersections: Architectural histories and critical theories* (pp. 221–246). London: Routledge.

Brooks, C. (2012). Space and consequences: The impact of different formal learning spaces on instructor and student behavior. *Journal of Learning Spaces, 1*(2). Retrieved from http://libjournal.uncg.edu/index.php/jls/article/view/285/275

Casey, E. S. (1997). *The fate of place.* Berkeley: University of California Press.

Edquist, H., & Grierson, E. (2008). *A skilled hand and cultivated mind: A guide to the architecture and art of RMIT University.* Melbourne: RMIT.

Foucault, M. (1979). *Discipline and punish: The birth of the prison* (A. Sheridan, Trans.). New York, NY: Vintage Books.

Foucault, M. (1991). Nietzsche, genealogy, history (D. F. Bouchard & S. Simon, Trans.). In P. Rabinow (Ed.), *The Foucault reader: An introduction to Foucault's thought* (pp. 76–100). London: Penguin.

Gray, B. (2011). *An old kiwi reminiscence.* Retrieved April 4, 2014, from http://winsomegriffin.com/Newsham/Barbara_Grierson.html

Ingraham, C. (1998). *Architecture and the burdens of linearity.* New Haven, CT: Yale University Press.

Manning, J. (2011). *Interview with Jack Manning.* Retrieved October 5, 2012, from http://www.nzia.co.nz/news–media/jack-manning-is-the-latest-recipient-of-nzia-gold-medal.aspx

Mitchell, D. (1984). *Kaleidoscope.* [Episodes 1–6] The elegant shed, March 9, 1984–April 4, 1984. Auckland: TVNZ Television Archive.

Nietzsche, F. W. (1983). *Untimely meditations.* (R. J. Hollingdale, Trans.). Cambridge: Cambridge University Press.

Openshaw, R., & Ball, T. (2006). New Zealand teacher education: Progression or prescription. *Education Research and Perspectives, 33*, 102–123. Retrieved from http://erpjournal.net

Rendell, J. (2006). *Art and architecture: A place between.* London: I. B. Tauris.

Salter, D., Thomson, D. L., Fox, B., & Lam, J. (2013). Use and evaluation of a technology-rich experimental collaborative classroom. *Higher Education Research & Development, 32*, 805–819.

Senior, K., & Dixon, M. (2009). Reading with the ancients: Embodied learning and teaching to an embodied pedagogy? *Access: Critical Perspectives on Communication, Cultural & Policy Studies, 28*, 21–30.

Shaw, L. (2006). *Making a difference: A history of the Auckland college of education 1881–2004.* Auckland: Auckland University Press.

Sturm, S., & Turner, S. (2011). 'Built Pedagogy': The university of Auckland business school as crystal palace. *Interstices: Journal of Architecture and Related Arts, 12*, 23–34.

Trussell, B. (1981). *Auckland teachers college: Reflections on a hundred years of teacher education.* Auckland: Centennial Committee of Auckland Teachers College.

Vail, H. (2011). *100 New Zealand world war one memorials 1914–2014.* Retrieved April 6, 2014, from http://100nzmemorials.blogspot.co.nz/2011/03/walter-alexander-grierson-mt-eden.html

Artwork as Technics

MARK JACKSON

Abstract

'Artwork as technics' opens discussion on activating aesthetics in educational contexts by arguing that we require some fundamental revision in understanding relations between aesthetics and technology in contexts where education is primarily encountered instrumentally and technologically. The paper addresses this through the writing of the French theorist of technology, Bernard Stiegler, as well as extending Stiegler's own discussion on the work of Martin Heidegger concerning the work of art and technology. Crucial to this discussion is recognition of the thinking of the late eighteenth-century German poet, Friedrich Hölderlin, on the work of Heidegger. The paper questions whether such recognition also extends crucial aspects of Stiegler's own thinking.

Introduction

This special issue of Access, 'Activating aesthetics', asks how 'the poetic or aesthetic' might be discovered and applied in educational scholarship and creative works. How do we activate an aesthetic sensibility? A grounding premise for this paper is that currently education is conceived, developed and practiced in overtly instrumental ways. Education is essentially conceived of as means to a broad spectrum of ends, increasingly driven by technologies that, themselves, emerge instrumentally. In this light, a call for activating an aesthetic sensibility is a call for bringing such instrumentalism into question, firstly by recognising or disclosing it and then by strategic or tactical adjustments that enable us to think pedagogical agencies poetically.

For this reason, the paper commences with introducing our most orthodox understanding of aesthetics, or poetics, which is to say the work of art derived from Kantian critique in Kant's *Critique of judgement* (1986). However, the paper asks if our most conventional and accepted understandings of the work of art, to be opposed to instrumentalizing technology and technoscience, are any longer relevant. Perhaps we need to equally ask how today we understand aesthetics and poetics. What Kant devised in terms of the moral image of the world may well have undergone a paradigm shift over the past 200 years. This paper suggests we now need to encounter a question of aesthetics, technology and education via the mediating field of ecology, that the question of the human, and *paidos*, the emerging human, is one that radically revises how we now come to understand technology's relation to aesthetics. The paper pursues this question via the work of Bernard Stiegler on technology, ecology and the human, that itself activates the work of Martin Heidegger on technology and the work of art. However, the paper commences with defining Kantian aesthetics.

The Moral Image

In the conclusion to his *Critique of practical reason* (Kant, 1997, pp. 133–134), Immanuel Kant suggests that human being possesses two realms, two possible worlds: that of the infinity of worlds within worlds, inspired by gazing at the starry sky, and that of a moral law within each human being. Radically and infinitely exterior and radically and infinitely interior, there are two possessions of the human that together construe our possibility to be. Yet, it might also be the case that it is not we who have this doubling-possessing as much as it is we who *belong* to this exteriority and interiority. It is we who are possessed by this double. For Kant, this doubling established the human as other than other beings. Kant draws a distinction between our finite animal being, as a creature that is eventually returned to the earth, and human being as intelligence, independent of the sensible world and extending to the infinite. With this distinction between a finite sensible world and an infinite intelligible world, is recognised a version of the dilemma that led Kant to formulate his notion of the *moral image* of the world. On the one hand, our reason strives for self-interested happiness as a maximum satisfaction. The pursuit of this idea leads to increasing disorder in the impossible coexistence of self-interests. On the other hand, there is the moral law as a *disinterested* order as maximum accordance among all imaginable actions, an order beyond our knowledge, where a supersensible being, a deity becomes the guarantee of our happiness, no longer determinable within our self-interested will:

> This enables us to accept our situation, namely, that we cannot even imagine in what our happiness could possibly consist. Our hope will now be directed toward an order beyond our knowledge—toward another dimension of our lives. Of it we know only that it must be a realm where a deity guarantees the appropriate distribution of happiness and moral merit. We have arrived at the *moral image*. (Kant, 1997; cited in Henrich, 1992, p. 21)

Kant's original understanding of the moral image of the world was transformed in the writing of his *Critique of practical reason* (1997) and *Critique of judgement* (1986), though it constituted an essential ground for his understanding of aesthetic judgement and human freedom. The work of art for Kant was, strictly speaking, without purpose, without finality or end, without rule in its making and without determinate or objective judgement in the universality of judgements of taste. Though, to be more precise, the Faculty of Judgement is nonetheless the faculty whose a priori principle is finality of nature: 'This faculty, with its concept of a finality of nature, provides us with the mediating concept between concepts of nature and the concept of freedom …' (Kant, 1986, p. 38). As independent of all interest, judgements of taste are absolutely subjective, without cognitive determination or recourse to desire or will. Such judgements are absolutely indifferent to the question of the real existence of the world:

> Now, where the question is whether something is beautiful, we do not want to know, whether we, or anyone else, are, or ever could be, concerned in the real existence of the thing, but rather what estimate we form of it on mere contemplation (intuition or reflection). … One must not be in the least prepossessed in favour of the real existence of the thing, but must pre-serve complete indifference in this respect, in order to play the part of the judge in matters of taste. (Kant, 1986, pp. 42–43)

Perhaps, and perhaps for some time now, we have come to understand the Kantian moral image—that which mediates between romantic nature and human freedom, what Kantian aesthetics sought to address especially in those things human-made that we yet call 'beautiful' and 'sublime'—under a new logic or *logos*, that of a particular *oikos* or dwelling, within the system of living things, what we currently name *ecology*. This new name for the moral image appears at that moment when *physis* and *tekhne* are inseparably written, when *tekhne* and *aesthesis* are reciprocally constituted and when *episteme* and *tekhne* emerge as technoscience. Such an *eco-aesthetic technology of nature* has emerged, on the one hand, within the panoply of critical engagements with vitalism and affect determined by both life-world phenomenology and Spinozist immanentism as counter-measures to neo-Kantian science and, on the other hand, via critical engagements with technology and technical determinism, again via legacies that are broadly phenomenological as well as Spinozist. And, crucially, ecology, as a science of life-world systems is a pedagogy inasmuch as it at once places the human within a systemic structure of life and, as a 'moral idea' constitutes by this systemic structure regulatory procedures for guiding the human as living being. We initially turn to questions concerning technics as a way of broaching the *tekhne* of an *oikos* that houses *paidos*, the emergent human—which is to say, *anthropos* as self-showing *tekhne*.

Tekhne & Tropes

It is now 20 years since the publication, in France, of Bernard Stiegler's *Technics and time, volume 1: The fault of Epimetheus*, (1998) the first of a three-volume work on rethinking an ontology of technology and the technical object. More recently, Stiegler has embarked on another three-volume work, titled *Disbelief and Discredit*, with vol-ume one—appearing in 2004—titled, *The decadence of industrial democracies* (2011). This latter work opens with a perspective on technological modernity that was simply not the concern of the *Technics and Time* volumes, a perspective that could be termed, in its brevity, the 'culture industries'. Stiegler emphasises that 'an industrial model of production and consumption has failed' (Stiegler, 2011, pp. 3–4), and it is necessary to radically think 'a renewed idea of this object' (4) which currently takes the form of 'structurally cultural capital' (4). Stiegler notes:

> It is in the first place a matter of giving a critique of the classical industrial model that was elaborated in North America long before the hyper-industrial

capitalist epoch. And yet, and principally to overcome what Marx called its 'contradictions', this classical model soon places cultural control at the heart of the process through which it pursues its development. This has not been generally understood by twentieth-century analysts of capitalism (with the possible exception of Gramsci and certainly of Adorno), and it has been made especially unthinkable, after 1968, by the sociological fable of the 'leisure society', also called 'post-industrial society'. (Stiegler, 2011, p. 4)

If I suggest that the key themes in *The decadence of industrial democracies* are not those of *Technics and time*, it is especially so in that the latter, for all of its funda-mental questioning of technology and the human, does not concern itself with, broadly speaking, the cultural and, in particular, with aesthetics. And it is not as if aesthetics is especially addressed in *The decadence of industrial democracies* either, though the question of aesthetics as that which becomes subsumed under a 'culture industry' may well be considered. This is an aesthetics whose production and consumption, emergence and dissemination cannot be dissociated from the most contemporary information and communication technologies, and a culture industry that has a pedagogical, educative and cohering force in normalising regimes of the social. Equally, the normalising techniques of educational practices, their housing and programmes have been developed precisely on these same determinants that construed the production–consumption models of culture industries. Education, in this sense, is a culture industry. Yet, it is Stiegler's *Technics and time: The fault of Epimetheus* that most essentially, though *indirectly*, points to some fundamental con-siderations of technics, time and aesthetics, or rather recognises how a transforma-tive encounter happens with what might once have been termed 'aesthetics'. In fact, it is curious that Stiegler does not explicitly address the work of art in this volume, as if he, too, was afflicted with the fault of Epimetheus—forgetting. I men-tion this in particular, as this volume, concerning an essential forgetting, is struc-tured around a 'confrontation' that Stiegler develops between Martin Heidegger's thinking on the essence of technology, in particular Heidegger's understanding of *Gestell*, discussed by Heidegger in 'The question concerning technology' (1977), and three key twentieth-century thinkers of technology and technics, Bertrand Gille, André Leroi-Gourhan and Gilbert Simondon.

On two counts it is surprising that the question of the artwork or poetics does not arise in this text. The most direct one is that it is precisely Heidegger who, in 'The question concerning technology', swings the whole conversation around from a con-cern with the devastating situation of the 'greatest danger', to be found in the stand-ing reserve of all things for a productionist metaphysics of 'challenging forth' what is, as raw material for production, to a 'saving power' to be found in an ontological counter-sway to a 'bringing-forth' of what is as *poiesis*, essentially a work of art. Stieg-ler takes us along the path of Heideggerian thinking on the essence of technology, only to uproot us from this path prior to encountering the radicality of Heidegger's understanding of the work of art, a radicality that makes a complete break with modernity's philosophies of aesthetics. One aim of *this* article is to pick up the scent of this path again, while keeping the radicality of Stiegler's understanding of technics and time in view. The second 'count' is, in a sense, the more intriguing one, as it implicates the whole thesis of the book, or at the very least, the originary moment out of which the book emerges. This concerns Plato's condemnation of the Sophists, thereby establishing the rivalry between *episteme* and *tekhne*. Stiegler reads this rivalry as decisive for Western metaphysics' determination of the binary and hierarchical difference between natural beings and all that is construction. It opens the radical space for his rethinking of technology and instrumentalism.

For Plato, the Sophists undermined philosophy's unequivocal determination of truth. For the Sophists, *logos*—language—was rhetoric, an art of speaking in tropes. Argumentation was tropic construction, and hence *tekhne*, and not the exposition of *logos* as true knowledge—*episteme*. Moreover, *episteme* is an end in itself, truth, just as natural beings have immanent to them movement, rest and growth; they, too, are their own ends. *Tekhne*, on the other hand, is not an end in itself, but a know-how for which many different ends are possible. Equally, no construction is an end in itself but a means for an end to be found in a natural being. Technical beings—constructions of all kinds—are means for ends which are not their own. Stiegler does not mention *poiesis* at this point, though could well have mentioned how Platonic philosophy likewise devalued the work of art, as it did *tekhne*, when compared with *episteme*. Stiegler notes:

> No form of 'self-causality' animates technical beings. Owing to this ontology, the analysis of technics is made in terms of ends and means, which implies necessarily that no dynamic proper belongs to technical beings. Much later [towards the end of the eighteenth century], Lamarck distributes physical bodies into two principal fields: the physiochemistry of inert beings; and secondly, the science of organic beings. ... To these two regions of beings correspond two dynamics: mechanics and biology. Lodged between them, technical beings are nothing but a hybrid, enjoying no more ontological status than they did in ancient philosophy. (Stiegler, 2011, pp. 1–2)

Stiegler's concern is radical: 'The object of this work is technics, apprehended as the horizon of all possibility to come and of all possibility of a future' (ix). For Stiegler, possibility is understood as opening to a futural becoming, hence a temporalizing of temporality. That opening's coming-into-view, its horizon, is technics. Technics *is* the horizon of temporalizing. But the efficacy of Stiegler's reference field, commencing with Heidegger, is to develop what is meant by that peculiar 'object'—technics. Technics is not technology understood as technical objects, nor *tekhne* understood in an ends-means distinction. Nor is technics anthropocentrically determinable. Stiegler understands this in a going-along-with Heidegger's 'The question concerning technology'. For Heidegger, the essence of technology is 'nothing technological', but rather a mode of revealing how the being of beings is disclosed otherwise than in the beings that are. How are beings disclosed in their being? In the epoch of technicity, as the culmination of Western metaphysics, which from the outset with Plato was productionist-metaphysics, beings are disclosed as a stockpile for production that is for-the-sake-of production itself. Human beings, too, are resources for production. For Heidegger, thinking this from the late 1930s, production is a planetary and systematic framework of ordering beings for production, a framing he terms *Gestell* —'enframing', also translated as 'apparatus', a systematic *challenging-forth* of what is. Education is to be thought as such a challenging-forth, a stockpiling of resources, human and otherwise for the sake of calculable production, economic ordering, and productive capabilities. Heidegger's essay of the mid 1930s, 'The origin of the work of art' (1993c), concerns the disclosure of artworks conventionally understood as standing reserve for an art industry: 'Works of art are shipped like coal from the Ruhr and logs from the Black Forest ... Beethoven's quartets lie in the storerooms of the publishing house like potatoes in a cellar' (Heidegger, 1993c, p. 145). As such a stockpiling, artworks are discussed as things revealed essentially as equipment, whose essence is reliability: in this sense indistinguishable from technical objects in contexts of an art industry or culture industry. Crucially, for Heidegger, while technical artefacts and a technical apparatus devastate the planet, the essence of technology, revealing the being of these beings, as the revealing of the greatest danger, oblivion of the planet, *as a revealing* also shows, in *Gestell*, the possibility for something other than beings disclosed as stock-piling for production.

While Stiegler does pursue a particularly Heideggerian understanding of temporality, in Heidegger's disclosure of the temporalizing of Dasein, from *Being and Time* (1986), he does not *fully* pursue Heidegger's thinking on the revealing of the essence of technology, of the saving power and recourse to the work of art. In short, he omits, or forgets to mention the sheer importance of the German poet, Hölderlin, in Heidegger's thinking, and the key role Hölderlin plays in Heidegger developing a transformative understanding of aesthetics as poetics. Instead, Stiegler systematically pursues the work of Gille, Leroi-Gourhan and Simondon, in order to develop more slowly with the successive refinements of their thinking of the object of technics, from Gille to Simondon, a radical encounter with the shifting thinking of ecology in an ever increasing inseparability of thinking *physis*—nature—outside of *tekhne* and thinking *anthropos*—the human —no longer as final cause. In discussing Simondon's understanding of the milieu of technical objects as adaptation and concretization, Stiegler notes:

> The technical object submits its 'natural milieu' to reason and naturalizes itself at one and the same time. It becomes concretized by closely conforming to this milieu. This ecological phenomenon may be observed in the informational dimension of present-day technics, where it allows for the development of a generalized performativity (for example in apparatuses of live transmission and of data processing in real time, with the fictive inversions engendered therein)—but it is then essentially the human milieu ... that is found to be incorporated into a process of concretization ... (Stiegler, 1998, p. 80)

Stiegler emphasises that with Simondon, the concretization of technical objects is not a 'humanization of nature', but rather will more readily appear as a 'naturalisation of the human' (81). That is to say, we tend to think of technical objects, as things fabricated by humans as an increasing transformation of nature—what is self engendering —into a humanization. Simondon's radical ecology considers this quite differently. Technics refers to the relational life of technical systems into whose ecology humans are increasingly embedded such that humans are increasingly understood as subjects of or subjected to a lifeworld of technics. In this, Stiegler's aim is to determine a 'saving power' in Heideggerian *Gestell*, not through the counter-sway of *poiesis*, but through a more radical determining of *Gestell*, as the temporalizing of technics. This is no longer humanism, nor even an anthropocentrism. That is, *Gestell* as a revealing of the disclosure of beings as a standing reserve also discloses how time as mediation may be thought differently, opening to Heidegger's concerns with ecstatic temporality. The second half of *Technics and Time* engages technics as that which will be thought along with Jacques Derrida: precisely as the Derridean *gramme*, the object of Derrida's early seminal text *Of grammatology* (1974) which deconstructs the very binary *physis/ tekhne* (Stiegler, 1998, pp. 137–142). Stiegler's engagement with technics and temporality opens the possibility for a radical considering of aesthetics and the pedagogical dimensions of aesthetics that would have recourse to neither an instrumentalism nor an anthropomorphism or anthropocentrism, where Kantian aesthetics understood as *mediation* between nature and human freedom will be radically rethought as immediation, immediacy, which is to say, as the absolute, thought as temporalizing temporality. Just what this infers is now pursued in relation to what Stiegler did not explicitly discuss in *Technics and time*: Heidegger's recourse to the German poet, Friedrich Hölderlin. But in doing so we need to address again the metaphysical distinction Stiegler emphasises between *episteme* and rhetoric or *tekhne* as fabrication.

Trope's Affections

There is an oblique parallel to be drawn between Stiegler's emphasis on Plato's distinction between episteme and rhetoric and a recent book on GWF Hegel, that reads this philosopher of the science of logic somewhat against the grain of orthodox interpretations. Katrina Pahl's *Tropes of transport: Hegel and emotion* (2012), presents Hegelian sophistry, the tropic movements of the Hegelian text whose affective register is no longer the self-identity of a coincident immanent transcendence of an I, but rather an affective emotionality of an impersonal textuality as auto-*poesis* (Hegel, 1977). Pahl introduces the *stimmung*—moods—or emotions of love, fear, despair and grief, not in terms of an Hegelian discourse *on* emotion, which does appear in the Phenomenology, and elsewhere in Hegel's writings, but in terms of what Hegel precisely does not make thematic. Pahl, like Stiegler, engages the rhetorical rather than epistemic structures of Hegel's production, emphasising an affective rather than logical ground. Hegel is transported in the very movements of his textuality by tropic shifts.

However, to recognise precisely such a reading of Hegel, a Hegel between emotion and reason and an 'alternate temporality', requires definitive reference to Hölderlin, the young Hölderlin who was a 'classmate' of both Hegel and Schelling, and who introduced to Hegel the thinking of Heraclitus, a thinking of an essential *polemos*, struggle or strife in all things, that led Hegel to thinking dialectics as such. It is also the Hölderlin whose river hymns, *The Rhine* and *The Ister*, are transporting tropes, concerning a passing through the foreign in a perennially homeless journeying homewards. These were the themes of lecture courses delivered by Heidegger in 1936

(Heidegger, 2014), and in 1942 (Heidegger, 1996b). Pahl suggests in her doctoral thesis on which her book publication is based:

> I locate the origin of speculative logic in the idea of love that Hegel develops in his early fragments. My analysis approaches Hegel's speculative thinking by way of Holderlin's turn to 'conversation' in the poem *Andenken* while discussing Holderlin's term *Andenken* (remembrance) in dialogue with Hegel's notion of *Erinnerung* (recollection). The communication that love affords is also invoked in the confrontation of Hegel's notion of experience with Kant's theory of aesthetic judgment. (Pahl, 2001, p. 2)

Tekhne's Uprootedness

Hölderlin developed a radical reading of Greek cosmology, wherein he saw in the Greeks a new beginning, and it is this new beginning that is the inception for Heideggerian thinking of the essence of technology, and it is this new beginning that Stiegler aims to pronounce in a radical discerning of temporality and technics that fundamentally *absents* the human. Hölderlin emphasises remembrance, recollection and forgetting, the tropic registers by which Stiegler reads the gods, Epimetheus and Prometheus. These references to remembrance and rhetorical fabrication suggest how aesthetic judgement is transformed in and through Stiegler's text, but with an indirection that may well be posing something radical with respect to understanding the work of art in its relation to technical objects. A 'new beginning' refers to Hölderlin's understanding of a radical caesura or break as absence within the ground of human existence. It concerns a radical sense of dwelling and belonging—*autochthony*—and of *ecology* in Stiegler's sense:

> Hölderlin's approach to autochthony includes a heightened sensitivity to matters of *terra incognita*, the absence within the ground of human existence. He refuses to absolve the tragic negation of consciousness through the successive steps of a dialectical system, contrary to his friends Schelling and Hegel. Hölderlin would rather preserve the crypt of nothingness by not allowing its abysmal rift to attain closure. He articulates the tragic negation as a caesura, the self-differentiating scission within language itself, which opens into the difference of word, metrical rhythm, even the poet's confrontation with the surrounding world. Caesura becomes most apparent between the heartbeats of poetry, in the silent spaces of the cadence of meter, at its line breaks, and anywhere else in which the 'sign' of poetry equals zero. This 'counter-rhythmic rupture' demonstrates the power of poetry to preserve difference in suspended equilibrium, without resolving, absolving, or dissolving the negation. (Nichols, 2009, p. 3)

Hölderlin's poetry is violent rupturing *against* the gods' determining powers as the force of nature, where the human is an excessive inwardness, ecstatically uprooting itself from rootedness, perennial dwelling in tropic foreignness, constituting a discordance between nature and freedom marked in the caesura. This tropic poetics is in

Stiegler's sense a technics, opposing any totalizing notion of *episteme* as a self-enclosing end. And, yet, this caesura is a dismantling discordance, a rupturing of homeland. Heidegger will come to understand this 'poetically man dwells' in the *polemos* or strife between earth and world, discussed in 'The origin of the work of art', where 'earth' is necessarily encountered in the context of Hölderlin's autochthony, as uprooted rootedness—earth is self-withdrawing jutting into world. Nichols, when discussing Heidegger's reading of Hölderlin's *The Ister*, will critique Heidegger for misrecognizing or overvaluing autochthony as rootedness and homeland, as if there is only a narrow preserve between Greek and German, to the exclusion of what was the very passing through of the foreign that constituted Greek soil in the first place (10). Stiegler says something similar concerning Heidegger and autochthony in a long footnote appearing in the second half of *Technics and Time* (Stiegler, 1998, p. 287). As with Nichols, this concern inflects on Heidegger's politics. Where Nichols contrasts Heidegger's discussion of Hölderlin's *Antigone* in his 1935 lectures, *An Introduction to Metaphysics* (2000), that emphasises *polemos*, strife and conflict, to his 1942 lectures on *The Ister* that shifts tone to *gelassenheit*, or a letting-be, Stiegler remains focused on the 1935 lectures, though emphasises something essential throughout Heidegger's thinking from *Being and Time* (1996a) to 'Building, Dwelling, Thinking' (1993b). Heidegger does not think uprootedness, un-earthing, essentially or primordially as *tekhne*:

> [Heidegger] will never have thought time from out of *prometheia*, an absence translated into the conflict that opposed *dike* and *tekhne*. The latter admittedly appears *in* and *as deinon*, but *tekhne* is never considered as the source of un-earthing/making-strange qua good un-earthing, not that of being torn away but that of returning to the most strange, to the most far, which is always the most familiar, concealed by its everydayness. (Stiegler, 1998, p. 287)

But for Heidegger to do so would essentially be to give the name *tekhne* to that strife between earth and world that constitutes 'truth happening in the work': precisely the work of art. And thus, in this sense, Stiegler did not see it necessary to bring Hölderlin's 'saving power' in 'poetically dwelling' into discussion, as already Stiegler, in a radical gesture, figures *tekhne* as coincident with the work of art, as the uprooting from dwelling, from the *oikos* of a *logos* we today name *ecological*, of a human ecology, as the making-strange or most uncanny of what is closest. As Stiegler emphasises, what most needs to be thought 'today more than ever' is that 'originary tension' between the *chthonian* and uprootedness precisely as an articulation between technics and time, 'conceiving technics as the very source of *de-paysement* in the insoluble complexity of its effects' (288).

Though, in his 1941 lecture course, *Basic concepts* (1993a), Heidegger interprets a fragment from the pre-Socratic Anaximander that precisely brings into proximity *dike*, normally translated as 'justice', along with what comes into being and what passes away. The name Heidegger gives to being, radically thought here, is 'enjoining' and to *dike* he gives the translating interpretation 'fit' or need. For what comes into being and for what passes away, both are an enjoining as a bringing forth, unconcealing a being in what it is, its 'fit'. In this sense, we might well ask to what extent can

Heideggerian being, as enjoining, be radically thought as *tekhne-poesis*, or more radically, as *physis-tekhne-poesis*? This throws light on the initial premise made at the commencement of this paper, concerning the instrumentalism predominant in the technological drivers of education and questions concerning an activating of an aesthetic sensibility. That 'sensibility' would not be a refusal of technological imperatives nor even a refusal of instrumentalism but rather an unconcealing, in Stiegler's terms, of what is closest as uncanny, uprooting the very familiarity of our everyday. And, in Heidegger's terms, disclosing the ontological dimension of technology as a mode of revealing and not simply an instrumentalizing means to an end. It is this 'strife' in discerning an ontological difference that opens to the poetic or aesthetic, thinking the being of what is 'fitting' as poetics. We would revise or rethink Kantian aesthetics, or judgements of taste concerning the finality of nature according to, on the one hand, Heideggerian thinking of *dike* as 'fit' in relation to being as enjoining and, on the other hand, in terms of Simondon's thinking of *tekhne*, nature and the human. That *paidos*, the emerging human, essentially the concern of pedagogy, would then be construed according to *logos* thought as unconcealing uprootedness rather than as logic. Our challenge is to recognise a transformative potential for education in such uprooting processes of 'making strange' in what is most familiar and to recognise, with Stiegler and Simondon, the life of technical systems as a radical poetics and radical 'naturalisation of the human'.

Disclosure statement

No potential conflict of interest was reported by the author.

References

Hegel, G. W. F. (1977). *Phenomenolbioogy of spirit*. (A. V. Miller, Trans.). Oxford: Oxford University Press.

Heidegger, M. (1977). The question concerning technology. (W. Lovitt, Trans.). In W. Lovitt, (Ed.), *The question concerning technology and other essays* (pp. 3–35). New York, NY: Harper Torchbook.

Heidegger, M. (1993a). *Basic concepts*. (G. E. Aylesworth, Trans.). Bloomington, IL: Indiana University Press.

Heidegger, M. (1993b) Building, dwelling, thinking. (D. F. Krell, Trans.). In D. F. Krell (Ed.), *Basic writings* (pp. 343–363). London: Routledge.

Heidegger, M. (1993c). The origin of the work of art, (A. Hofstadter, Trans.). In D. F. Krell (Ed.), *Basic writings* (pp. 139–212). London: Routledge.

Heidegger, M. (1996a). *Being and time.* (J. Stambaugh, Trans.). Albany, NY: State University of New York Press.

Heidegger, M. (1996b). *Hölderlin's hymn "the Ister".* (W. McNeill & J. Davis, Trans.). Bloomington & Indianapolis: Indiana University Press.

Heidegger, M. (2000). *An introduction to metaphysics.* (G. Fried and R. Polt, Trans.). New Haven, CT: Yale University Press.

Heidegger, M. (2014). *Hölderlin's hymns "Germania" and "the Rhine".* (W. McNeill & J. Ireland, Trans.). Bloomington, IL: Indiana University Press.

Henrich, D. (1992). *Aesthetic judgment and the moral image of the world.* Stanford, CA: Stanford University Press.

Kant, I. (1986). *The critique of judgement.* (J. C. Meredith, Trans.). Oxford: Oxford University Press.

Kant, I. (1997). *Critique of practical reason.* (M. Gregor, Trans.). Cambridge: Cambridge University Press.

Nichols, D. (2009). Antigone's autochthonous voice: Echoes in Sophocles, Hölderlin, and Heidegger. Retrieved October 24, 2014from https://www.google.co.nz/webhp?sourceid=chrome-instant&ion=1&espv=2&ie=UTF-8#q=David%20Nichols%20Antigone

Pahl, K. (2001). *Tropes of transport: The work of emotionality in Hegel's phenomenology of spirit.* University of California, Berkeley, ProQuest, UMI Dissertations Publishing, 3044619. Retrieved from http://search.proquest.com.ezproxy.aut.ac.nz/docview/304685003?pq-origsite=summon

Pahl, K. (2012). *Tropes of transport: Hegel and emotion.* Evanston, IL: Northwestern University Press.

Stiegler, B. (1998). *Technics and time, volume 1 the fault of Epimetheus.* Stanford, CA: Stanford University Press.

Stiegler, B. (2011). *The decadence of industrial democracies.* Cambridge: Polity Press.

Katsushika Hokusai and a Poetics of Nostalgia

DAVID BELL

Abstract

This article addresses the activation of aesthetics through the examination of an acute sensitivity to melancholy and time permeating the literary and pictorial arts of Japan. In medieval court circles, this sensitivity was activated through a pervasive sense of aware, *a poignant reflection on the pathos of things. This sensibility became the motivating force for court verse, and through this medium, for the mature projects of the* ukiyo-e *'floating world picture' artist Katsushika Hokusai. Hokusai reached back to* aware *sensibilities, subjects and conventions in celebrations of the poetic that sustained cultural memories resonating classical lyric and pastoral themes. This paper examines how this elegiac sensibility activated Hokusai's preoccupations with poetic allusion in his late representations of scholar-poets and the unfinished series of* Hyakunin isshu uba-ga etoki, *'One hundred poems, by one hundred poets, explained by the nurse'. It examines four works to explain how their synthesis of the visual and poetic could sustain* aware *themes and tropes over time to maintain a distinctive sense of this aesthetic sensibility in Japan.*

Introduction: *Mono no aware*

How can an aesthetic sensibility become an activating force in and through poetic and pictorial amalgams of specific cultural histories and memories? This article examines how the poignant aesthetic sensibility of *mono no aware* (a 'sensitivity to the pathos of things') established a guiding inflection for social engagements of the Heian period (794–1185CE) Fujiwara court in Japan. Its pervasive presence in Japanese culture survives to the present day. It can be provoked through observations on the passing of youth and beauty, and in ephemeral motifs of seasonal change, or snow, moon or blossoms (Shirane, 2012). This aesthetic consciousness generated sensitivities, informed codes of social intercourse and attitudes to nature, and most especially, it shaped the refined literary themes of the Heian age. A sensitivity to *aware* repeatedly provided the generating impetus to (and was, in turn, sustained by) the composition of medieval short verse (*waka*), and the word itself appears no less than 1018 times in Murasaki Shikibu's (*c.* 978-c.1014 or 1025) court novel *Genji Monogatari* (Morris, 1969). For the

75

nineteenth century artist, Katsushika Hokusai (1760–1849), the activating force of *aware* sustained through poetry provided the motivating themes of two late-career pictorial projects. The sustained memories of the sense of *mono no aware,* experienced through their poetic tropes, were to stimulate the development of his own deeply affecting and nostalgic constructions of bucolic worlds beyond the city. In these works, he was to meld the poetic and the pictorial in gently constructed syntheses of worlds of past and present. The following discussion examines this amalgam of the poetic and pictorial as an activating aesthetic sensibility in these later works of Katsushika Hokusai.

A Poet in Exile

The sense of *aware* informing classical verse inspired, and was maintained through, many of the themes adopted by Edo period (1615–1868) *ukiyo-e* ('floating-world picture') artists. Indeed, early Buddhist appreciations of *ukiyo* as 'this fleeting, sorrowful world' mirrored the sensitivities of *aware* itself. For Katsushika Hokusai, these themes were to provide perfect vehicles for the aesthetic preoccupations of his mature reflections on the poetic and the nostalgic. Between 1833 and 1834, Hokusai designed a series of 10 pictorial compositions on themes of great poets of earlier eras titled *Shika shashinkyô* ('A True Mirror of Chinese and Japanese Poets'). The Chinese-themed compositions include *Haku Rakuten,* a representation of the Chinese poet Po Chû-i, (772–846; Po Chû-i Wades-Giles; Bai Juyi, *pinyin*; Hakkyoi, or Haku Kyoi, Japanese); a poetic scene from the *Nô* play *Tokusa kari* (*Tokusa-gari*, or 'Peasant Carrying Rushes'); *Ri haku,* a portrait of the Chinese poet Li Po (701–762; Li Po, Li Bo, Wades-Giles; Li Bai, *pinyin*; Rihaku, Japanese); *Tôba,* the Chinese poet and calligrapher Su Tung-p'o (1037–1101; Su Tung-p'o, Wades-Giles; Su Dongpo, *pinyin*; Su Tôba, or Tôba, Japanese); and *Shônenkô* ('The Journey of Life'), illustrating a Chinese poetic theme of the young man setting out from home. The Japanese prints represent themes on the poets Minamotu no Tôru (822–889), *Tôru no daijin* ('The Minister Tôru'); Ariwara no Narihara (823–880); Sei Shônagon (fl. 1002); Abe no Nakamaro (698–770); and Harumichi no Tsuraki (fl. 920).

Hokusai's composition of the Japanese scholar Abe no Nakamaro is set in China. He has located the poet on a high patio overlooking the Eastern Sea between China and Japan, seated with three distinguished guests, with an attendant serving food and beverage. The foreground is dominated by an enormous perforated rock formation at lower right, a steep-pitched roofline behind it, and a tall branch of pine reaching right to the top of the composition. In the background, rocky outcrops extend into the sea towards a group of fishing boats. It is a deeply poignant scene; Nakamaro turns away from his guest and his servants, gazing wistfully out across the sea, towards a shining full moon hovering in the evening sky in the upper left.

This is a complex, layered composition. In one sense, it is an historical representation. The Japanese scholar-poet Abe no Nakamaro (701–770 CE) resided in China. He accompanied a priest, Genbô (d. 746), and the aristocratic scholar, later ambassador, Kibi no Makibi (695–775) on a study mission to China in 717. He remained there when the embassy returned in 718, subsequently sitting the Chinese civil service examinations and serving, under the Chinese name Chao Heng, in the administration of the T'ang Emperor Hsûan-tsung. He served in administrative posts in Luoyang, Chang'an and Hanoi until his death in 770. Nakamaro's enjoyment of the privileges of birth, education and position are evident in the rich setting and servants, in his fine brocade clothing, and in the delicate grace of his disposition as he turns to look towards the moon, and across the gulf that lies between China and his home. His privileged position and scholarly status seems to have brought him into contact with respected Chinese poets including Li Po (Li Bai) and Wang Wei (Mostow, 1996). Though he did maintain senior administrative positions on the mainland, Nakamaro's residency was effectively one of exile. Attempts to return to Japan in 734 and 753 were confounded by shipwrecks, and at times, his movements were constrained by periods of political instability. Consequently, Hokusai's composition reflects something of an ambivalence between the security of a man comfortable in his institutional status on the one hand, and one hopelessly longing for a return to his home on the other. Here, and in other compositions on the theme, Hokusai clearly locates Nakamaro on the Chinese mainland (Morse, 1989). Both the Chinese architecture and the perforated limestone rock formations are conventional indications of this setting (Figure 1).

Beyond its representation of a real figure in a Chinese setting, this composition is suffused with poetic allusions resonating feelings of loneliness and longing for home,

Figure 1: Abe no Nakamaro. From the series *Shika shashin kyō*, by Katsushika Hokusai, 1833–1834. Private Collection. Printed with permission

and sustaining broader seasonal themes and early Japanese aesthetic sensibilities. Associations of contemplative reclusion with poetic sensibilities also have long traditions in Chinese literary and art history, and the subject of the Chinese scholar-poet recluse has been a recurrent pictorial theme from early times. In Japan, the ideal of aesthetic reclusion and its associations with poetics, learning and wisdom had enjoyed a significant revival in *sumi-e* ink painting during the Momoyama period immediately preceding the Edo period of Hokusai's time (Brown, 1997). This revival established a firm, and immediately accessible, field of reference for Hokusai's own explorations of the theme.

Both Hokusai and Abe no Nakamaro were able to draw on an extensive stock of motifs from the natural world and its cycles of seasonal change to charge their pictorial or literary constructions with an acute sense of melancholy. Autumn (*aki*) and images of the autumn moon and autumn breeze had been associated with melancholic themes since as early as the compilation of the *Man'yôshû* ('Collection of Ten Thousand Leaves', post-759 CE), the oldest of the Japanese poetry anthologies. In poetry, 'autumn is associated with sorrow, sadness, personal frustration and a sense of mortality' (Shirane, 2012, p. 43). Thus, in a verse from the Imperial *waka* anthology *Kokinshû*:

Monogoto ni	In all things
aki zo kanashiki	autumn is sad
momijitsutsu	when I think of what happens
utsuroiyuku wo	when the tree leaves
kagiri to omoeba	turn colour and fade. [Autumn 1, No. 187]
	(Shirane, 2012, p. 43)

For Heian readers, this feeling of melancholy provoked a sense of *mono no aware*, an awareness of the pathos of things, or a sense of the mysterious depth of *yugen*, '... expressive of desolation and rich mysterious beauty coupled with sadness' (Miner, 1968, p. 165). The moon (*tsuki*) became a poetic staple for sorrow and pathos, as in this anonymous verse from the *Kokinshû*:

Ko no ma yori	When I see the light of the moon
morikuru tsuki no	leaking through the trees
kage mireba	I know
kokorozukushi no	the heart wrenching autumn
aki wa kinikeri	has arrived. [Autumn 1, No. 184]
	(Shirane, 2012, p. 41)

For Abe no Nakamaro, the image of the full autumn moon, rising simultaneously over both his present location and his home, is a poignant and nostalgic reminder of his isolation. The pine tree provides a clue as to the source of his reflection. A homophonic reading of *matsu* ('pine') as *matsu* 'to wait' generates associations with waiting, especially waiting for a lover:

Ume no hana	If the flower of the plum tree
sakite chirinaba	blooms and scatters
wagimoko wo	I will be the pine that waits
komu ka koji ka to	wondering if my beloved
aga matsu no ki so	will come or not come. [*Man'yôshû*, 10 1922]
	(Shirane, 2012, p. 137)

In Hokusai's composition, the association alludes to Nakamaro's love and longing for his home.

For Hokusai, these contemplative and melancholic themes of the past were to activate the aesthetic pre-occupations of his own Edo period present, realized through the pictorial medium of the *ukiyo-e* floating world prints of his time. These works could then, in their turn, re-activate those elegiac sensibilities for a new generation of viewers. Hokusai's creative purvey in these projects reached beyond the literary and pictorial pasts of his own Japanese world to embrace also models of Chinese precedent. The landscape subject and Chinese setting of his portrayal of these themes is complemented by his adoption of conventional Chinese pictorial constructions. The vertical *nagaban* (c. 25 × 56 cm) print format echoes the Chinese-style hanging scroll format, so popular, in Japan. The Chinese spatial convention of stacked 'zones' of water, architecture or foliage and warm and cool colour provides a cohesive structure in which the highest strata were understood to be further distant than those lower in the pictorial field. A sense of suspension, of floating, indicated in the fluid *bokashi* modulations of transparent hue and tone in the sea and sky and in the cantilevered architecture is also consistent with the fugitive forms and surfaces of Chinese scroll painting. The Chinese-style asymmetrical 'corner-directedness' of the composition is characteristic also of Japanese *shinsai* 'formal-style' painting. Within these conventional means, Hokusai is able to forge an intimate synthesis of Japanese sensibilities (*Yamato gokoro*) and Chinese sensibilities (*kara gokoro*) that linked poetic aesthetic tastes of his world with those of the ancient Nara and Heian courts. The naturalism of this conventional construction made it easy for Hokusai's pragmatic viewers to accept the imaginary reconstruction of a distant event as a real view on an actual scene. Like the verses on autumn loneliness, it is an idealized construct, a complex and richly allusive pictorial ideal of the poet-scholar in reclusion built around a poetic nostalgia for an idealized memory of Japan, refined Japanese sensibilities, and a lost world of aesthetic, literary and social elegance.

One Hundred Poets

For Hokusai, the mature career projects of the Fuji series and poetic and literary themes became centred on the construction of idealized pictorial worlds like those of the *Shika shashin kyô* series. In all of these works, Hokusai removes his pictorial interest away from the immediate urban subjects of the Edo 'floating world', to situate his figural engagements in bucolic rural settings. The synthesis of the poignancy of *mono no aware* with his deeply felt nostalgia for the aesthetic sensibilities of distant worlds became the activating theme of his final pictorial engagement with the poetic.

The major undertaking of a full set of illustrations for the *Hyakunin isshu uba ga etoki* ('One hundred poems by one hundred poets, explained by the nurse', c. 1835–1836) was never completed, though many of his designs survive as working drawings (Morse, 1989). Hokusai's compositions for this series fall into two groups: one of representations of the poets of the anthology, and the larger one in which its poetic themes are represented obliquely, in idyllic scenes of country life. All are removed from the city; their genre interest is located in coastal, mountainous, village settings or farming scenes consistent with the recurrent pastoral motifs of the *Hyakunin isshu* collection. Even those with Heian-kyô court subjects barely reveal the capital. Removing each view from the here-and-now of the city to rural locations also, implicitly, obscures the temporal distance between the 'now' of Hokusai's own viewers and the much earlier origins of the works in the anthology.

The original *Hyakunin isshu* anthology was compiled by Fujiwara no Teika (alt. Fujiwara no Sada'ie, 1162–1241) some time after 1239 (Herwig & Mostow, 2007). Successive publications maintained its popularity and exemplary status through to Hokusai's time. Abe no Nakamaro's poem, the earliest in the *Kokinshû* anthology, had been composed during the Nara period. Most of the *waka* in the *Hyakunin isshu* dated from the Heian period—Muneyuki's (Plate 4) from before his death in 983CE, and that of Sanjō In (Plate 3) from before his abdication in 1016. This 'blurring' of temporal distance must have enhanced the immediate appeal of classical themes for Hokusai's contemporary audiences, most of whom would have been well versed in classical literature. Removing each composition from a specifically identifiable time also effectively informed a degree of timeless universality consistent with the classic themes and status of the verses themselves (Figure 2).

For his illustration on Abe no Nakamaro, Hokusai draws on the same iconographic stock as that of the earlier composition. Here also he situates the principal figure on the Chinese mainland. He employs a similar, if more extensive, figure group, and again the poet's status is reflected in his fine brocades, and emphasized in the respect indicated by the two figures kowtowing to him. The same devices of pines and moon, (now reflected on the sea), emphasize themes of sorrow and loneliness and isolation from home.

The compositions for Hokusai's *Hyakunin isshu* are distinguished from the earlier series of Chinese and Japanese poets by the inclusion of the *waka* from the anthology, each inscribed in a square cartouche, over a stylized colour field suggesting layers of autumn mist. As in the earlier composition, Abe no Nakamaro is represented above the sea, standing on a hilltop, gazing longingly across the Eastern Sea towards Japan. Joshua Mostow's (1996) reading of Nakamaro's poem emphasizes its expression of melancholic isolation and wistful yearning:

ama no hara	As I gaze out, far
furi-sake mireba	across the plain of heaven,
kasuga naru	ah, at Kasuga,
mikasa no yama ni	from behind Mount Misaka,
ideshi tsuki kamo	it's the same moon that came out then! (p. 129)

Figure 2: Abe no Nakamaro. From the series *Hyakunin isshu uba ga etoki*, by Katsushika Hokusai, *c.* 1835–1836. Dunedin Public Art Gallery. Printed with permission

In retaining the quietly exclamatory 'Ah!' of earlier transliterations (Joly, 1908), Mostow preserves a suggestion of the poignant Heian period sensibility of *mono no aware* pathos (Morris, 1969). The suggestion links Hokusai's representation quite explicitly with aesthetic sensitivities to autumnal themes of sorrow, melancholy and loneliness of Heian taste. A commentary in an early version of the *Kokinshû* confirms that the poem was composed on the occasion of a banquet held in China on the eve of his attempt to return to Japan:

> Long ago, Nakamaro was sent to study in China. After he had had to stay
> for many years, there was an opportunity for him to take passage home with
> a returning Japanese embassy. He set out, and a group of Chinese held a
> farewell party for him on the beach at a place called Mingshou. This poem
> is said to have been composed after nightfall, when Nakamaro noticed that
> an extraordinarily beautiful moon had risen. (McCullough, 1985, p. 97)

A sense of occasion is illustrated explicitly in both of Hokusai's compositions, in the inclusion of distinguished guests, servant and banquet food in the earlier version, and here in the inclusion of Chinese officials and the gaily coloured banners and screens of a festive occasion.

Including the *waka* text invested Hokusai's representation with an explicit indication of the source of Nakamaro's sadness. The identification of both Kasuga Shrine and Mount Misaka (Wakakusa-yama, overlooking the old capital of Nara) maintained both nostalgic and spiritual allusions. The nostalgic reference emphasizes his poignant memory of the distant, earlier, time and place. Traditionally, pilgrims had prayed for their safe return at Kasuga Shrine. In comparing the moon he sees from the Chinese shore and that at Kasuga, Nakamaro is making a direct comparison between the moon he observed when praying at Kasuga on the eve of his departure in 717, and the moon he sees now (Mostow, 1996). The pictorial and poetic association emphasizes the wistful nostalgia of the Nakamaro theme.

In composing his *waka*, even during the eighth century, Abe no Nakamaro was able to draw on a catalogue of natural world subjects with established connotations. The associations of the moon and mists with autumn sadness and sorrow or the pine with waiting, longing and love were such conventional allusions. Over one thousand years later, Hokusai was able to draw on the same conventional iconographies as maintained through poetic and painting traditions, and in written commentaries and pictorial illustrations in volumes of the *Kokinshû* and the *Hyakunin isshu*. Mostow (1996), for example, draws on illustrations of Nakamaro from Hishikawa Moronobu, 1678, *Hyakunin Isshu Zôsan Shô*; Moronobu, 1695, *(Fûryû) Sugata-e Hyakunin Isshu*; an anonymous artist included in *A Hundred Verses from Old Japan*, by William N. Porter, 1909; and an anonymous 1749 Kyoto artist for Hakagawa Tsuneki's edition of the *waka* anthology *Man'yô Shû*.

The illustrators drew on a range of Nakamaro-appropriate staples. Unless the poet is represented with no background, the universal convention is for a shoreline setting, overlooking rolling waves on the Eastern Sea between China and Japan. The full moon is generally viewed shining in a patch of clear sky between layers of cloudy autumn mist. Though Hokusai's *Hyakunin* illustration has the moon in reflection on the calm sea surface, his earlier preparatory drawing follows the conventional sky setting (Morse, 1989). Nakamaro is generally represented wearing elegant decorative brocades of Nara period fashion, together with the rather awkward-looking black *hikitate eboshi* headwear, rather than the decorative *kammuri* style popular amongst the aristocracy. His companions may include other poet-scholar figures, typically bearded, or participants in the farewell celebration. Perforated rocks and rambling, tortured trees, often with creeper covered branches, signified the Chinese location of the poem's composition. In a number of illustrations, Nakamaro's outstretched, upturned hand alludes to the perfection of the moment; the whole scene held in his hand.

Though the pictorial constructions and stylistic modes Hokusai developed were remarkable in their day for their innovation and novelty, they still drew on these broadly accepted and understood traditions of representational devices. For poets and artists alike, these themes and subjects of the seasons, nature and human sensitivities to suffering informed the aesthetic construction of '…a largely harmonious universe in which nature … functions as an elegant and often highly nuanced expression of human thought and emotion' (Shirane, 2012, p. 54). Drawing on classical conventions and melding them with contemporary modes made these enduring subjects and subtly allusive themes accessible to new, and more pragmatic, audiences. Within this professional flux between convention and innovation, Hokusai, like Nakamaro before him, was constructing something of a nostalgic ideal that maintained poetic values of the past within his own Edo world (Figure 3).

Figure 3: Sanjô In. From the series *Hyakunin isshu uba ga etoki*, by Katsushika Hokusai, *c.* 1835–1836. Dunedin Public Art Gallery. Published with permission

Classical and Bucolic Ideals

This mutually activating interface of classical sensibility and poetic/pictorial means was also to galvanise Hokusai's aesthetic synthesis of court themes and rustic idylls in the landscape/genre compositions of this series. Some of his illustrations for the *Hyakunin isshu* contain time-specific references to the classical court of Heian-kyô (shrines, pavilions, ceremonies or celebrations); others are set in 'timeless' bucolic, rural settings far removed from the crowded urbanity of Edo. His *Sanjô In* composition belongs to the former group. Like Nakamaro's, Sanjô's *waka* turns on the *aware* sensibility of the melancholic alignment of suffering (Sanjô experienced chronic ill health), autumn, the passage of night and the moon:

kokoro ni mo	Though it is not what is in my heart,
arade uki yo ni	if in this world of pain
nagaraheba	I should linger, then
kohishikarubeki	no doubt I shall remember fondly
yoha no tsuki kana	the bright moon of this dark night!
	(Mostow, 1996, p. 343)

The first three lines refer to Sanjô's abdication at this time, and beyond this, suggest a longing for freedom from the painful shackles of life. The inclusion of the syllables *uki* and *yo*—together 'floating world'—evokes a sense of both his own suffering and of the original Buddhist meaning of *ukiyo* as this 'fleeting, sorrowful world'. Sanjô found his release in the following year.

Hokusai's illustration embraces both the nocturnal setting and the lunar emblem, clearly framing the latter just above and to the right of the centre of the composition. The *kumogata* bands of cloud forms intruding across from upper left and lower right are reminiscent of autumn mists and their allusions of sorrow and mystery. The setting is a Heian Shinto temple ceremony for the Shinto moon god (and brother of the Goddess Amaterasu) Susanô O no Mikoto (Morse, 1989). Coincidentally, Susanô is sometimes credited as the inventor of the 31-syllable *waka* form (Morse, 1989). The ceremony is held in autumn, on the 15th day of the eighth month. This autumnal subject evokes the deeply contemplative pathos of *mono no aware*. Together with its nocturnal context, it suggests something of the depth and mystery of *yugen*. This is reflected in the solemn dispositions of the figures themselves: the attendant priests and noblemen (beyond them to the right) are completely self-absorbed. There is no clear engagement between the figures, and none engage directly with the viewer. This avoidance of engagement is sustained throughout the series of designs of Hokusai's *Hyakunin isshu* series (Figure 4).

Like the *Sanjô In* illustration, Hokusai's composition for *Minamoto no Muneyuki ason* (Plate 4), is a nocturnal scene, but in a mountain landscape setting. Though the hunters and woodsmen are all animated, crowding around the same warming blaze, it seems difficult to locate any genuine sense of companionship or communication. Their words seem lost in the rising waves of smoke, silenced by the muffling layers of snow around them. Rather than fraternity, the picture seems to suggest isolation. This sense

Figure 4: Minamoto no Muneyuki Ason. From the series *Hyakunin isshu uba ga etoki*, by Katsushika Hokusai, *c.* 1835–1836. Dunedin Public Art Gallery. Printed with permission

of silence and loneliness is reflected in Lord (*ason*) Minamoto no Muneyuki's (d. c. 939) *waka*:

yama-zato ha	In the mountain village,
fuyu zo sabishisa	it is in winter that my loneliness
masarikeru	increases most
hito-me mo kusa mo	when I think how both have dried up,
karenu to omoheba	the grasses and people's visits
	(Mostow, 1996, p. 226)

Hokusai's setting and iconography conform to poetic and pictorial conventions for this theme. Snow (*yuki*) is the universal signifier of winter (*fuyu*), often closely linked with mountain settings like Yoshino-yama, Fujiyama, Shirayama or Atagoyama in *uta-makura*, scenes of places rich in poetic evocations of the past (Shirane, 2012). Pictorial iconographies for this verse include a secluded mountain village or sometimes a single humble cottage in a mountain valley (Mostow, 1996). These were also the standard settings, in Chinese and Japanese painting traditions, for scenes of scholastic and poetic reclusion. The isolation of hermetic life, introduced explicitly in the second line of the poem, is echoed poetically in the poignant analogue of its final two lines, and pictorially in the chill isolation of Hokusai's mountain scene.

Hokusai's compositional construction for *Minamoto no Muneyuki ason* complements these sensibilities. The frozen movement of his figures informs the sense of stillness and silence. Hokusai has emphasized this frozen moment by the articulation of a carefully wrought spatial tension evident in the complex three-dimensional construction in the exaggerated twist of each figure, and through the web-like interrelations of figures, fire, columns of smoke, branches and architecture right across the pictorial space. This interwoven tracery of diagonal dispositions acts against the stability of the horizontal layers of snow-covered ground, dark foliage behind the figures and the night sky above. The tension is enhanced further by the unusual spatial ambiguities Hokusai has constructed here. The interweaving branches of the trees at upper right, for example, appear alternately in front of, or behind, one another. This spatial ambiguity extends down through the arrangement of branches, trunks and snow-covered eaves to the bottom of the composition. In constructing this network of ambiguities, Hokusai was engaging in a kind of pictorial play that would have delighted his Edo audiences' taste for novelty and pictorial provocation. The effect also enhanced the allusive potentials of the pictorial composition in a way that complements those of the poem, and informs a degree of timelessness shared with so many of his *Hyakunin isshu* designs.

In this work, as in all of his compositions for the series, Hokusai avoids references to specific scenes in the city, or moments in his own time. Employing rural settings removed his subjects from the present, engaging his audiences in an intercourse with pastoral and bucolic themes now so completely removed from their own immediate urban experience that they had acquired something of a timeless quality. Hokusai's is a fondly expressed view on the past. His figures live in ideal harmony with their natural and rural surroundings in pastoral idylls, preoccupied in reflective contemplation of pines, water or moon, gracefully rising wafts of smoke or steam or the delicate pleasures of elegant dance and music. Even where they focus on the Spartan conditions of manual labourers, farmers, woodsmen, fisher folk or travellers, these are quiet, ideal worlds, far removed from the pragmatics of everyday life in the bustling mercantile centre of Edo. The distance, together with the idealism of his portrayals, generates a profound sense of nostalgia that complements the parallel idealism and timeless, universal themes of the *Hyakunin waka* of a thousand years before.

A Poetics of Means: Maintaining Conventional Practices of the Past

The activating force of these sensibilities was dependent on their intimate synthesis of conventional precedents of both verse and painting traditions. Both poets and artists forged their profession within clearly defined conventional parameters. The principal poetic form of the great anthologies was the 31-syllable *waka*, or *tanka*, 'short poem' format of five lines, arranged in a sequence of five, seven, five, seven and seven syllables. This structure suited the closely melded synthesis of a small range of motifs (moon, snow and pine) and sensibilities (*aware* loneliness or sorrow, or in love poems *yōen* romantic ethereal beauty (McMillan, 2008)) in highly allusive combinations. Within these constraints, poets developed delicately wrought variations on classical subjects, themes and wordplays.

Typically, a *waka* might be conceived and constructed in response to, and as a subtle variation on, an earlier or contemorpary verse.

Donald Keene, for example, explains how, while arranged within the same conventional structures of *waka* verse, a composition by the court poet Lady Sagami (998-before 1061) could turn on the same sentiments, word constructions and subjects as a near contemporary poem by Fujiwara on Michimune (d. 1084) (Keene, 1956, pp. 24–25). Both poets build through the same word images of perennial emblems of *aware* pathos, the vulnerable under leaves of lespedezas, the arrival of autumn, and the cold autumn winds blowing across the moor. They differ only in their selections of two plaintive motifs: in Michimune's verse, of crying quail, and in Sagami's, of the crying of young deer. Sagami has added one further delicate refinement, an enduring emblem of the crystal beauty, but ephemeral fragility, of the gathering dew in the chill morning air. As Keene notes, the two poems are essentially the same, in their structure and in their suggestiveness around complementary sentiments and motifs. They are distinguished only by the inflections of elegant rephrasings, shaped by the subtly differing sensibilities of their individual composers.

Conforming to the same structural modes ensured the 'serial unity' (McMillan, 2008, p. xxx) or maintenance of stylistic consistency over time, and informed the compositions of the Heian *waka* poets with a degree of elegance, economy and restraint. Building from common sensitivities, using complementary language and emblems, maintained a consistent aesthetic sensibility. In a similar way, Hokusai's dependence on conventional formal means informed the structural cohesion of his designs and the naturalistic credibility of their landscape and genre views. A balance between informational sufficiency, economy (especially in comparison to later Edo pictorial extravagance) and restraint generated a degree of elegance commensurate with the poetic forms. The small *ōban* (26.5x39 cm) print format lent the pictorial medium an intimacy consistent with that of the *waka* verse form.

Though Hokusai's diverse training endowed him access to a wide variety of conventional modes, the compositions of the *Hyakunin isshu* draw most heavily on both Chinese precedents and *Yamato-e*, or distinctively Japanese modes of representation, of the classical Heian traditions of the poets. Chinese-style 'perspective' conventions included spatial arrangements of 'stacked' strata of landscape motifs. Hokusai combined these interlocking constructions of diagonally alternating forms and spaces with the asymmetrical 'corner-directed' principles of *shin* 'formal' painting. He employed the full diversity of Chinese-style mark-making and linear modes (Bowie, 1952) in all their descriptive and allusive varieties to construct pictorial surfaces visually consistent with the elegant calligraphies of the poems. The empirical naturalism of the *Hyakunin isshu* compositions conforms to Chinese injunctions to observation from nature, and controlled mastery or 'freshness' (*sheng*) of skills promoted by painter-scholars like Ku Ning-yüan (Hua Yin; fl. 1780; Lin, 1967) or restraint and the avoidance of vulgarity advocated by Shen Tsung Tien (Chieh-chou; Hsüeh Hua P'ien; fl. 1781; Lin, 1967).

By Hokusai's time, these Chinese-sourced modes had been thoroughly assimilated into the painting styles of *Yamato-e* ('national', or distinctively Japanese pictures) and later *nanga* ('Southern-style', i.e. Chinese), Tosa and Kanô school paintings. *Yamato-e* models informed Hokusai's adoption of isometric orthogonal projections for architectural constructions, as in the architectural forms of the earlier Nakamaro scene, and the internal architectural space in the *Sanjô In* composition. These solid, clearly defined volumes provide a stable pictorial structure, and a measure for the interpretations of scale and interaction in genre scenes. In *Sanjô In*, Hokusai has also employed the *fukinuki yatai* 'roof-blown-away' convention of viewing the architectural construction from above, as though the roof and sometimes a wall were removed, to provide a clear view on the figural interaction within. For this composition, Hokusai also employs the *Yamato-e* convention of flat, stylized cloud bands, or *kumogata*, to frame the architectural and figure construction between intrusions of the cloud-like bands from left above and from the right below. The device coincidentally pushes the pictorial scene back, separating it from the viewer's world, emphasizing its situation in an earlier era.

Hokusai's landscapes in this series are, often broadly conceived, expansive. The figures that populate them are necessarily small, yet Hokusai was able to animate them, informing a lively sense of activity in his rural genre scenes. The old-school *hikime kagibana* nose and eyes convention suited Hokusai well here. It informed a singular degree of descriptive vitality in tiny facial constructions, and it sat well beside the rich descriptive variety of Kanô School brush stroke Hokusai applied to a diversity of linear, textural and dynamic effects. These effects were often contained within the rich and precise contours of *Yamato-e* painting. They were also combined with the softer definition of edges of tonal or colour surface in the *mokkotsu* or 'boneless' style (i.e. without linear contour) of the Japanese Tosa school painters. The Tosa painters had also maintained the polychrome style of *Yamato-e*. Again, Hokusai adopted the colourful diversity to enliven his pictorial surfaces, and to invest them with a credible naturalism consistent with *Yamato-e* convention and with the ways people could view the landscape and its people themselves. Importantly, and again consistent with *Yamato-e* precedents, however, idealised they may be, each pictorial subject of the *Hyakunin isshu* scenes is distinctly Japanese in focus, if not (in the case of the Nakamaro work) in setting.

In these works, and in his other mature works, Hokusai was not constrained to work within these conventional modes; he chose them to suit his purpose. Elsewhere in his oeuvre, he employed a rich range of other contemporary modes, including the perspectival representational devices of the Western painters evident in some scenes in this series. The taut, twisting Katsukawa School single-figure types of Hokusai's teacher Shunshô provide models for the sturdy hunters of *Minamoto no Muneyuki ason*. The rising columns of smoke above them are relieved by the stylized rhythmic linear decoration of Rinpa school origin. In both of the Nakamaro compositions, a western-style diminution of scale generates the deep spatial projection that tangibly emphasizes Nakamaro's impossible distance from his home. Most importantly, however, these other conventions complement the effectiveness with which the fundamental conventional modes of Chinese and *Yamato-e* derivation inform the convincing realism, structural coherence and pictorial credibility of Hokusai's inventive constructions around themes from the past.

What is remarkable about Hokusai's *Hyakunin isshu* series is the seamless synthesis of such diverse sources and conventional means, and the cohesive way in which he melds these with the classical poetic tropes of his sources. Hokusai's pictorial constructions balance convincing representations of human and natural world subjects with elusive *aware*-infused poetic tropes and literary themes from a thousand years before. They closely complement the intense visuality of the verses themselves (McMillan, 2008). Hokusai's cohesive crystallisation of the conventional economies of poetic means and aesthetic sensibilities with the expansive pictorial methods at his own disposal generated a coherent sequence of poetically charged pictorial compositions accessible by the entirely new middle-class audiences of the later Edo period.

Conclusion

In engaging in this pictorial project, Hokusai was motivated by *aware* sensibilities of the poetic classics that had been sustained for almost one thousand years. These sensibilities found expression in poetic and pictorial appreciations of nature, realised in *utamakura,* poetically significant landscape settings (mountains, caves, rocks and waterways, in Shinto traditions the locus of spiritually significant phenomena), or motifs rich in conventional associations—the moon, pine trees, bamboo or willow (sorrow, longevity and integrity, strength and flexibility and resilience, respectively). Many made explicit reference to sites of special cultural and spiritual significance— Mount Misaka, Kasuga Shrine or the Heian-kyô Fujiwara Court. Hokusai's compositions embraced aesthetic virtues of *aware*, humility and 'symbolic poverty' (Brown, 1997, p. 73) resonating sensibilities favoured in *chanoyu* (the way of tea) and craft traditions, and consistent with Chinese injunctions to humility, simplicity and the 'avoidance of vulgarity' of Shen Tsung Tien (Lin, 1967, pp. 201–202). These informed the wholesome simplicity of Hokusai's motifs of rural life, honest manual labour, simple *sôan*-style rustic dwellings or themes of scholarly retreat or aesthetic reclusion (Brown, 1997). The nostalgic significance of these subjects, themes and sensibilities found their most appropriate expression in Hokusai's adoption of formal conventions of *Yamato-e* and Chinese-sourced traditions.

Hokusai's engagements of *aware* were framed through nostalgic views on the past; his Heian themes and landscape/genre compositions construct poetically charged and idealised views on times, themes and habits that lay beyond the immediate experience of his Edo audiences. In sustaining these themes, Hokusai became an active agent in the maintenance of aesthetic habits of cultural ('collective' and 'social') memory, the amalgamation of social, material and cognitive memories through which individuals and communities mediate the relations between their present experiences and those of the past (Erll, 2008). Mnemotechnical devices of places, objects, behaviours, ideologies, physical or imaginative sites—*loci memoriae*, or *lieux de mémoire*—provided the means through which significant cultural memory could be sustained (Boer, 2008); *aware* sensibility provided its motivating impetus. In Heian Japan, the poetic anthologies themselves had provided effective vehicles for this function. These metaphorical 'media of memory' (Assmann, 2011) had found poetic expression in the motif of a 'floating bridge of dreams' (*yume no ukihashi*) or as 'pictures of the heart' (Mostow, 1996). Haruo Shirane adopts the phrase 'traces of dreams' to describe the fugitive elegance of these aesthetic sites in his study of the haiku poetics of Matsuo Bashô (1644–1694). In Hokusai's day, the *utamakura* poetic landscape topography (Shirane, 1998) provided geographical sites; poetry clubs and their *za* gatherings or *uta-awase* poetry contests offered social sites; *waka*, *kyōka* 'crazy verse', haiku and *ukiyo-e* provided literary and pictorial aesthetic loci for the mediation of experiences of *aware*.

Underpinning the late reflective projects informing Hokusai's engagements with the poetic, bucolic, ephemeral, melancholic or nostalgic lay this motivating but elusive sensibility of *mono no aware*. Its pervasive presence infected his projects more profoundly than any contractual obligation. In his illustrations for *Abe no Nakamaro* or *Sanjō In*, he was constructing poetically charged aesthetic sites of cultural significance in refined pictorial form, drawing selectively from precedents, means and sensibilities of the past. He was building on the graphic stock of cultural and aesthetic memory through which Heian, Kamakura, Muromachi or Momoyama audiences had made sense of and maintained the histories, manners, and above all, the poetic sensibilities through which they maintained their elegant tastes and sense of social and aesthetic identity. Hokusai's was a carefully contrived vision, an *aware*-infused nostalgic and pastoral idyll of an ideal past. Projects like the *Hyakunin isshu* could maintain these culturally significant memories in ways that revived this poignant sensibility anew for the audiences of his own world.

References

Anonymous. (1968). *Tales of Ise: Lyrical episodes from tenth-century Japan* (H. McCullough, Trans.). Stanford: Stanford University Press.

Assmann, A. (2011). *Cultural memory and Western civilization: Functions, media, archives.* Cambridge: Cambridge University Press.

Boer, P. (2008). Loci memoriae–lieux de mémoire [Locations of memory – sites of memory]. In A. Erll & A. Nünning (Eds.), *Cultural memory studies: An international and interdisciplinary handbook* (pp. 19–25). Berlin: Walter de Gruyter.

Bowie, H. (1952). *On the laws of Japanese painting: An introduction to the study of the art in Japan.* New York, NY: Dover.

Brown, K. H. (1997). *The politics of reclusion: Painting and power in Momoyama Japan.* Honolulu: University of Hawai'i Press.

Erll, A. (2008). Cultural memory studies: An introduction. In A. Erll & A. Nünning (Eds.), *Cultural memory studies: An international and interdisciplinary handbook* (pp. 1–15). Berlin: Walter de Gruyter.

Herwig, H. J., & Mostow, J. S. (2007). *The hundred poets compared: A print series by Kuniyoshi, Hiroshige, and Kunisada.* Leiden: Hotei.

Joly, H. (1908). *Legend in Japanese art.* Rutland: Charles E. Tuttle.

Keene, D. (Ed.). (1956). *Anthology of Japanese literature: Earliest era to mid-nineteenth century.* Rutland: Charles E. Tuttle.

Lin, Y. (1967). *The Chinese theory of art: Translations from the masters of Chinese art.* London: Panther Books.

McCullough, H. C. (1985). *Kokin wakashū: The first Imperial anthology of Japanese poetry.* Stanford, CA: Stanford University Press.

McMillan, P. (2008). *One hundred poets, one poem each: A translation of the Ogura hyakunin isshu.* New York, NY: Columbia University Press.

Miner, E. (1968). *An introduction to Japanese court poetry.* Stanford, CA: Stanford University Press.

Morris, I. (1969). *The world of the shining prince.* Harmondsworth: Penguin.

Morse, P. (1989). *Hokusai: One hundred poets.* London: Cassell Publishers.

Mostow, J. (1996). *Pictures of the heart: The Hyakunin isshu in word and image.* Honolulu: University of Hawai'i Press.

Shirane, H. (1998). *Traces of dreams: Landscape, cultural memory, and the poetry of Bashō.* Stanford, CA: Stanford University Press.

Shirane, H. (2012). *Japan and the culture of the four seasons: Nature, literature, and the arts.* New York, NY: Columbia University Press.

Thoughts on Film: Critically engaging with both Adorno and Benjamin

LAURA D'OLIMPIO

Abstract

There is a traditional debate in analytic aesthetics that surrounds the classification of film as Art. While much philosophy devoted to considering film has now moved beyond this debate and accepts film as a mass art, a subcategory of Art proper, it is worth reconsidering the criticism of film pre-Deleuze. Much of the criticism of film as pseudo-art is expressed in moral terms. Adorno, for example, critiques film as 'mass-cult', mass-produced culture which presents a 'flattened' version of reality. Adorno worries about the passivity encouraged in viewers. Films are narrative artworks, received by an audience in a context, making the focus on the reception of the work important. The dialogue held between Adorno and Walter Benjamin post-Second World War is interesting because, between them, they consider both the possible positive emancipatory and negative politicization effects of film as a mass produced and distributed storytelling medium. Reading Adorno alongside Benjamin is a way to highlight the role of the critical thinker who receives the film. Arguing that the critical thinker is a valuable citizen, this paper focuses on the value of critical thinking in the reception of cinematic artworks. It achieves this by reconsidering Adorno and Benjamin's theories of mass art.

Introduction

Much of the current philosophy of film literature pursues an optimistic approach that may be identified with Walter Benjamin's hope for the art of the masses. This optimism sees film as a vehicle for screening philosophical thought experiments, offering new perspectives on issues relevant to everyday life by engendering critical consciousness. If films allow for philosophical thinking, then they encourage social, political and economic critique of social norms. Yet, most popular films that are digested in large quantities are Hollywood or Bollywood blockbuster films that are generally criticized for depicting stereotypes and for eliciting formulaic emotions (Collingwood,

1969, p. 57). Theorists who conceive of cinema as a means of thinking must first reply to the objections that most films are formulaic and do not encourage active, intelligent or imaginative participation. Prior to the publication of Deleuze's cinema books (1986, 1989), theorists such as Adorno feared the advent of the Hollywood Studio film as akin to Nazi propaganda. Dismissed as elitist, Adorno's concern was that mass-produced and distributed artworks portrayed social norms as immutable reality. If the viewer's imagination cannot enter and engage with messages depicted through the filmic medium, then viewers cannot critique the moral and social status quo as screened; instead, they simply receive it and the depicted stereotypes are reinforced. Audiences may be able to engage critically with such narratives, yet the focus on the reception of the narrative screened is worth considering in further detail. In this paper, Adorno will be read alongside Benjaminesque theories of film, in order to focus on the critical attitude of the viewer, as well as the moral messages of the film. While there are many different stories being told in contemporary culture, the focus on the critical thinker, the interpreter of the narrative, is vital.

If critical thinkers are important for society and films as mass art can engender a critical reception, then Adorno's concern for uncritical ingestion of mass art would be valid. Although Adorno may have overstated his concern, his desire for critical reflection of mass art appears to be well placed and is a sentiment shared by Benjamin. As Hansen notes:

> Abandoning his defensive stance against the cinema as a mass media, Adorno can even conceive of a 'liberated' film which would have to 'extricate its a priori collectivity from the mechanisms of unconscious and irrational influence' and enlist it 'in the service of emancipatory intentions.' Benjamin would not have disagreed. (1981–1982, p. 192)

Film, as a technological art form, can be viewed and understood by many people virtually on first contact (Carroll, 2004, pp. 486–487) and can elicit powerful responses. The nature of these various responses is still under debate, but includes responding to the emotional quality of films, their images and realistic representations (Wartenberg, 2007, p. 5) that can depict various aspects of society, character and politics. Following Carroll, I shall use the term 'mass art' to refer to mass-produced and distributed artworks such as film. On Carroll's definition (1998, p. 196), film is art *qua* art, yet it may not be very good (both aesthetically and ethically). Following the influence of Deleuze, much of the current philosophy and film literature is optimistic with regards to the potential of films to explore philosophical ideas. The cinematic experience is powerful because it combines sensory input with story to convey social, political and emotional truths. Colman illustrates this in her claim:

> The audio-visual nature of certain cinema … achieves 'a victory' over th[e] heirarchization of modes and concepts of art. This is also a victory in philosophical terms for art as a political form that contributes something to the world. (2011, p. 253)

This idea that film can provide a social commentary and thus be meaningful, as opposed to mindless, is an aspect of the contemporary Deleuzean approach to film that reflects the optimism that emerges from Benjamin who celebrates the potential of films to screen ideas. Yet, the stronger claim that can be read from Benjamin's writings that critical detachment is somehow built into mass media because audiences watching films are distracted (Benjamin, 1969, p. 240) should be reconsidered. Adorno and Horkheimer warn of the less desirable aspects of cinema such as the passivity of its viewers and its economic motivation. These concerns need to be considered alongside Benjamin's celebration of cinema. Neither Benjamin nor Adorno and Horkheimer are completely correct; yet, both hold value and are relevant to reconsidering important ethical aspects of film spectatorship.

Osborne and Charles remark that, "the ecstatic character of Benjamin's political thought at the outset of the 1930s, sees technology appear on a political knife-edge between its possibilities as 'a fetish of doom' and 'a key to happiness'" (2011). Film, when fetishized, is focused on making money or promoting an ideology rather than telling stories as a narrative art form. Carroll notes, 'Perhaps the greatest anxieties about mass art concern morality' (1998, p. 291) and Benjamin points out that, for example, fascism can pervert the natural tendencies of mass art (1969, pp. 243–244). Yet there should be a reconsideration of the stronger claim that can be read from Benjamin, namely, that mass art has 'natural tendencies' that are emancipatory. We can see that film may be motivated by economic reasons as well as ideological ones when we consider the numerous sequels of, for example, *Fast and Furious* which are enthusiastically received by mass audiences.[1] It is useful to re-examine and juxtapose Adorno and Horkheimer's view with Benjamin's. In doing so, we are reminded of the ability film has to manipulate and be used as an economic and political apparatus, as well as a vehicle for harmless entertainment and, possibly, insight and even wisdom. Even though Adorno does not envision the potential and possibility of film in the way that Benjamin speculated and Deleuze celebrated, his concerns should not be dismissed. Film, as an art of the masses, embedded within society and used by social, political, moral humans, has the potential to be constructive *or* destructive.

Benjamin acknowledges the potential for mass art to manipulate, yet he contends that mass art is progressive in its ability to transform human perception, not by expressing or emblematizing it, but by encouraging its evolution (Carroll, 1998, p. 122). For Benjamin, film allows the viewer to stand outside of it, critically. This is due to the camera work as mediator between actor and viewer that 'permits the audience to take the position of a critic, without experiencing any personal contact with the actor' (Benjamin, 1969, pp. 228–229). As an aside, the influence of Bertolt Brecht and Sergei Eisenstein in this approach is critiqued by Adorno who is wary of Benjamin's use of these theorists in supporting a strong claim about the emancipatory power of film (Osborne, 2008, p. 63). From Benjamin, we learn that the power of film may be harnessed once we have recognized the mechanisms of the apparatus (Benjamin, 1991, pp. 107–108). As noted, Benjamin's theory does not discount film being used either to empower *or* to attempt to monopolize viewers with images depicted en masse. Osborne and Charles (2011) note that Benjamin's writings on film are justly renowned for their twin theses of the transformation of the concept of art by its 'technical reproducibility' and the new possibilities for the collective experience this contains, in the wake of the historical decline of the 'aura' of the work of art, a process that film is presented as definitively concluding. While this more traditional art aura regresses, there is also the chance, Benjamin suggests, of a newly liberated 'distracted' viewer who is progressive, keeping up with new, active filmic techniques (Markus, 2001, p. 17). Yet, Adorno's concern that the new media will lead to a dystopia or even the collapse of civilization should give us pause to think more deeply about the impact of mass art on viewers.

For Adorno, who is concerned with the aesthetic value of unique artworks, the loss of aura is not cause to celebrate; the technologically reproducible artwork is not as valuable because it does not challenge the viewer to actively engage with the picture of society it presents. In this way, mass artworks are unlike so-called 'high' or avant-garde artworks and thus, lack ethical as well as aesthetic value. Adorno and Horkheimer state, 'The double mistrust of traditional culture as ideology is combined with the mistrust of industrialized culture as a swindle' (p. 161). Adorno has been criticized as being elitist and his writings on jazz certainly do nothing to defend him from this claim (McCann, 2008, pp. 12–13). However, it must be noted that the sense of value to which he refers is not simply aesthetic, but also social and political. With the benefit of hindsight, if we acknowledge that Adorno was overly critical of the medium of film and overstated his ethical and social concerns with regards to the passivity of viewers, some of his critique is still salvageable and relevant to the contemporary debate about film and philosophy. Furthermore, it is important to take the conversation in its context of Hitler taking control of Germany in the 1930s and the Nazi effort to eliminate avant-garde art that challenged the political picture of the Weimar Republic they wished to sustain. Having witnessed the effect of propaganda in Nazi Germany and moving to America to form the Frankfurt School, Adorno and Horkheimer bore witness to the rise of the Hollywood Studio Film system in Post-Second World War America. Writing in the 1930–1950s, they worried about the ethical impact of the culture industry on society and the lack of diverse narratives being screened. While the current social and political climate is much changed, their focus on the moral impact of engaging with mass-produced and distributed products of a media industry is still of relevance today. The alleged lack of value (aesthetic and ethical) and the promotion of negative values (e.g. hyper-nationalism) of mass-consumed artworks require examination, even if not all films are guilty of Adorno's criticisms. Instead of dismissing Adorno as a naysayer whose critique of film restricts the possibilities for creative expression via a technologically reproducible medium, a re-reading of Adorno is timely with respect to the moral consideration and social importance of this popular form of art.

The writings of both Benjamin and Adorno are relevant in our technological society with its blurry lines between art, media and technological sharing platforms and social networking sites. We can value the different stories being told in contemporary culture, but we must also be mindful of the context in which these stories are conveyed and received. If films are powerful tools for communication, then we may convey many diverse messages through the power of story. The viewer's uptake of such messages may be constructive or destructive, as the creative force has the potential for both. An obvious example of this is the fine line that separates propaganda from entertainment whereby we cannot always tell the difference in product or affect.

Directors have the ability to encourage a positive (life-affirming) or a negative (life-denying) response to people, events and the earth itself: ranging from Disney and Michael Bay's proclamations of 'save the world!' to Lars Von Trier's attitude of 'let it all explode'. With this in mind, I propose we reconsider film spectatorship by re-reading Adorno alongside Benjamin.

Where is the Place for the Thinking Viewer in the Cinema?

This optimism of the power of film to think and encourage thinking is taken up by contemporary theorists like Thomas Wartenberg, who see film as a vehicle for screening philosophical thought experiments and offering new perspectives on issues that (may) have relevance to everyday life. Wartenberg claims that 'film is able to give philosophical concepts and ideas a human garb that allows their consequences to be perceived more clearly' (2007, p. 5) and, 'films can *make arguments, provide counterexamples* to philosophical claims, and *put forward novel philosophical theories*' (2007, p. 9). If films allow for philosophical thinking, then they are like some other so-called 'high' artworks, in that they encourage social, political and economic critique of social norms. If contemporary films depict diverse narratives instead of constructing a homogenous picture of social reality, then audiences are encouraged to think critically by imaginatively engaging with multiple perspectives, thereby alleviating Adorno's fear of passivity. Yet, Adorno's (albeit overstated) concerns are still worthy of discussion. Many, if not most, popular films that are digested in large quantities promote stereotypes with dubious moral values. Wartenberg is correct to claim that some films are philosophical, yet he gives examples of Hollywood blockbusters to support his claim though it is mostly these films that are subject to the Adornian criticism. Hollywood blockbuster films that are screened ubiquitously and make the most revenue are the kinds of mass produced and distributed works to which Adorno objects. Theorists who conceive of cinema as a means of thinking must still reply to the objection that most films simply do not encourage active, intelligent, imaginative participation with the stereotypes therein depicted. While this does not demolish claims that films can somehow 'do' philosophy, the acknowledgement that film may encourage critical reception must not discount the caution offered by Adorno.

Wartenberg acknowledges how realistic and convincing the depictions are through the filmic medium; yet, he doesn't acknowledge the criticism of this very same quality. For Wartenberg, the lifelike quality of films allows the viewer to be absorbed in the narrative. Yet, it is this same feature that results in many blockbuster films resisting imaginative engagement by presenting their story in a manner so all-inclusive that there is less room to imagine it differently. Most blockbuster films depict stories in approximately 90–120 min, tying up loose ends in order to leave a feeling of resolution with the viewer. The viewer is not given the time to reflect on the story while watching it, as they may do when reading a book, which adds to the sense that the story is immutable. A screened story is designed to be ingested as a whole, is usually less complex than a novel and invokes base emotional responses such as revenge, sadness, romance etc.without encouraging any critique of the context that elicits these feelings (Levine, 2001a, pp. 63–71). Film is almost always designed to be accessible.

While this in itself is not a bad thing, accessibility often means that detailed argument is lost and 'watered down' due to the compressed nature of film. Admittedly, films do not have to be simplified in this manner, but many, particularly blockbusters, are and these are the most watched films. Even Wartenberg acknowledges that structural avant-garde films:

> are made for a small, intellectual audience, not for the huge audience that Hollywood films aim to reach. As a result, they are more hermetic, harder to watch and understand, and call for a very different type of attention than do standard fiction films. (2007, p. 117)

From Wartenberg's comment, it may be discerned that in contrast to avant-garde films, blockbusters are designed to be easier to watch and understand, precisely because they are targeted at large audiences. It is accepted that there are auteurs, who knowingly engage with philosophical ideas and portray them through film, yet cannot 'do philosophy' without the audience actively participating in the experience and reflecting on the ideas presented. The quote above also makes mention of the kind of attention called for, from the spectator, to appropriately receive the film. I would suggest that viewers watching films philosophically, and those watching philosophical films, are already critical thinkers, which explains their attraction to philosophical films requiring of them this 'very different type of attention'. A crucial aspect of film's *raison d'être* is to be seen, engaged with and received. If only some films allow for critique of social, political and economic norms and these films are attended by critical viewers, then how is film more generally a tool for thinking? It must be acknowledged that Hollywood blockbusters attract a large proportion of cinema-going audiences and these blockbuster films are unlikely to attract critical thinkers.

Wartenberg acknowledges this criticism and replies as follows with reference to Charles Chaplin's *Modern Times* (1936):

> Still, the objector might persist, even if you are right about that, viewers do not watch the Chaplin film for its philosophical insights, but for its humour. Although you might be able to squeeze some philosophy out of its portrayal of the assembly line, we are not interested in the film for that, but rather for Chaplin's amazing antics. Here, I can only agree that Chaplin's comic riffs are an important source of our interest in *Modern Times*. But I would go on to point out that the humour of the sequence I have been discussing is intimately bound up with the thought that the human being is functioning as a machine, mechanically ... As I see it, you cannot separate the film's serious thinking about alienation from its comic portrayal in order to deny that the film involves a philosophically significant contribution. (2006, p. 30)

Wartenberg claims that in order to understand the film and appreciate its humour, you are already thinking about the philosophical concepts of human and machine. Yet, the viewer may not reflect on arguments about industrialization in order to laugh at the film and, as such, they may not be 'doing philosophy'. In order to be 'doing philosophy', surely the viewer has to be aware that they are thinking about the philosophical concept under discussion. If there is no reflection on a concept—in this instance, on the concept of mechanization and the human as automaton, then this is not an instance of philosophical thinking. Wartenberg is suggesting that to understand the humour, you also understand the concept philosophically, i.e. of human as automaton. However, if philosophical thinking is broadened out as Wartenberg here describes, then family resemblance is lost and any kind of mental activity that involves thinking becomes 'doing philosophy'. Philosophy, in this way, ceases to be recognized as reflective thinking that involves considering arguments, counter-arguments and responses. As we have already seen, Wartenberg acknowledges these elements are important to philosophy. While some films may be able to philosophize in this manner, if the spectator is not aware of the arguments being made, can it be claimed that the spectator is doing philosophy simply by laughing at the images depicted? Whether or not this claim is upheld, it returns us to Adorno's suggestion that the focus on the viewer is of relevance to critical engagement with mass art.

What We Can Learn from Adorno

Prior to the publication of Deleuze's cinema books, theorists like Adorno and Horkheimer feared the advent of the Hollywood Studio film as akin to Nazi propaganda. Dismissed as elitist, their concern was that mass-produced and distributed artworks portrayed social mores as immutable reality. If the viewer's imagination cannot critically engage with film, i.e. through montage or similar 'shock' techniques, then viewers cannot critique the moral and social status quo screened; instead, they simply receive it and it is reinforced. Concerned that technology within a capitalist framework allows for mass-produced and distributed artworks to be formulaically churned out, creating a culture industry, Adorno claims in 'Culture Industry Revisited':

> although the culture industry undeniably speculates on the conscious and unconscious states of the millions towards which it is directed, the masses are not primary, but secondary, they are an object of calculation; an appendage to the machinery. The customer is not king, as the culture industry would have us believe, not its subject but its object. (p. 13)

Adorno's hostility towards the culture industry is evident but times have changed and, as Thomas Wartenberg notes in the preface to his *Thinking On Screen: Film as Philosophy*:

> I am struck by a sense of arrival ... for the field of film and philosophy. When I began to argue that films could be relevant to philosophical concerns, that claim was met with a rather stony silence in the world of Anglo-American philosophy.

Yet, amongst this relatively new-found enthusiasm for film by analytic philosophers, it must be acknowledged that much of mass produced and distributed art is primarily aimed at commercial success as opposed to encouraging critical spectatorship. Often appearing to promote equality and challenging the existing social, class and racial discriminations, when critically examined, the messages of most Hollywood productions is one of the status quo that encourages viewers to passively accept the depicted version of social values.

Defining values as generalized, with cross-situational dispositions acting in certain ways, Brummett claims that values can show through form in film, even without the medium being exclusively linguistic (2013, p. 62). Films convey values to the audience through the way they conclude a narrative; depicted images and scenes; and enhance mood through lighting, sound and visual effects (Brummett, 2013, p. 66). Relying on the notions of homology as tied to ideology, Brummett explains that:

> This idea of homology can be a way to understand how texts may appeal to values without ever linguistically articulating them. Predispositions to respond to and to judge, socially held guides for choices, all the things that values 'are', may be activated at a formal level. This is not the same thing as being brought to conscious awareness, because we are so often not fully aware of how form is working in our texts and our experiences. Like ideology, form is most powerful when it is most invisible, and that is most of the time. (p. 64)

Brummett suggests that we read films through their formal features in the same way we read and understand social contexts. Films are lifelike and viewers have a shared understanding of social expression which comprises non-verbal as well as linguistic conventions. As such, we communicate and gather meaning, including values, from film in much the same way as we do in everyday life. For example, the first scene in a romantic comedy where the protagonist meets or sees the character with whom they will eventually form a romantic relationship will be shot in a certain way with specific music and lighting and the body language of the characters will indicate to viewers that this is the relationship we are watching to see how it unfolds (which is, often, predictably). This ideal of a 'soulmate' may then play out in the film suggesting that the ideal relationship is one that overcomes odds and ends 'happily ever after'.

Adorno was concerned about the homogenizing effect of the culture industry which depicted specific social and moral messages. Adorno did not allow space for critical engagement with mass artworks. In creating products for consumer consumption, Adorno claims that the mass-produced and distributed artworks are all different, yet all the same, creating a homogenized product that is willingly ingested by the masses. Adorno explains:

> Illusory universality is the universality of the art of the culture industry, it is the universality of the homogenous same, an art which no longer even promises happiness but only provides easy amusement as relief from labour. (Adorno & Horkheimer, 1997, p. 7)

Adorno's concern does not apply to every film, yet there are certainly formulaic and homogenous stories told and re-told through mass artworks. If we consider the Hollywood blockbuster romance films and apply Brummett's technique of reading the patterned rhetorical messages throughout a few of them, we reach this same conclusion. Whereas Brummett claims the message is not explicitly argued for, he details readings of films that give rise to certain values embedded in the form of the films (p. 67).

This is evident in romantic comedies that have a predictable plot line of girl meets boy, girl is not interested in boy, there is an event that causes them to have to work together in some manner and they eventually fall for each other, only being reunited and professing their love at the last minute after encountering a number of obstacles designed to separate them. The values of 'true love conquers all' and the idea of taking a 'leap of faith' as love is only truly love if you have to risk something in order to pursue it are common themes in such films. The interesting question is what, if any, affect do such stories have on viewers?

Certainly, Adorno overstates his claim and his view is too extreme, as evidenced when he writes that even those viewers attempting to engage with mass art actively or critically, are only ever enacting a pseudo-active voice and are doomed to ineffectual rebellion against such stories. Adorno writes, 'whenever they attempt to break away from the passive status of compulsive consumers and 'activate' themselves, they succumb to pseudo-activity (1997, pp. 52–53).' Adorno here is referring to acts of rebellion such as 'writing letters of complaint' that are ineffectual against the mass culture industry. These days, however, there is much power to be had in the voice of the dissatisfied consumer who makes use of social media in order to express their perspective. The viewer can be critical and express an active voice. However, despite his lack of recognition of the power of the individual spectator, Adorno's belief that mass consumerism forms an economic urge to create easily digestible works for the lowest common denominator must not be disregarded. The 'rom-com' is a case in point. The viewer may be critical of the film's story, yet is likely to have the relevant emotions at the end when the couple finally overcome adversity and admit their love for each other. As the music swells, there is a close-up of two smiling faces and even the cynical viewer is moved. They may not apply this belief in soulmates to their own life, but they may feel the burden of the stereotype each time they are asked why they 'aren't married yet' or when they are 'going to settle down'.

Adorno first claimed in *The Culture Industry* that the masses seek and love the rules by which they are bound through buying in to mass cultural commodities and their associated ideals. It is certainly the case that the culture industry has acquired and maintained immense social, political and economic power. Even when we knowingly engage with products of this culture industry such as Reality TV, gossip magazines, sartorialist street style blogs and relentless twitter feeds, are we not still buying in to that machine? Adorno is wrong to claim that the viewer is almost always completely passive and cannot counter the narrative and its associated values screened. However, as Brummett details, the subtle messages of values and ideology are screened and do reinforce existing social values. Brummett explains:

> Values are rarely, if ever, explicitly articulated in the films, and if they are, is it in the context of arguments about how to deal with instant rabies rage virus [i.e. science fiction or fantasy films that may have a clear ethic explicitly screened]—hardly the sort of relevance one encounters in everyday life. Yet I think the homology obtained across the films, the audience's experience of the medium, and the audience's experience of the strange urban context likely invokes a sense of values and their application. (p. 66)

Brummett's explanation of the homogenized messages and values that pervade films is tied to the understanding that films are created by social, moral and political people and companies. Likewise, there is an understanding of the seemingly obvious point that the reason viewers understand films is because they too understand the social context of which they are also a part. This more subtle reading of how film influences viewers is compatible with the ethical concern described by Adorno. Although Adorno's original thesis is too strong, his worry is still recognizable in film spectatorship today.

Adorno's point to be remembered is that films are created in a political, social and economic context and they influence the society which sustains them. One aim of Hollywood films is to keep the attention of mass audiences in a bid to retain their economic contribution. One way this is achieved is by not challenging certain stereotypes that attract mainstream and widespread audiences. These stereotypes have imbedded values linked to ideological contexts. While there is room within the dominant capitalist ideology for diversity, capitalism seeks to remain dominant and therefore does not allow *a great deal* of diversity. As Adorno observes, the value of creative autonomy is the expression of diverse perspectives. This idea is summed up by Osborne, who writes, 'the idea of creative autonomy here is an ethical idea rather than a substantive notion: a regulative ideal rather than an accomplishable goal' (2008, p. 9). Adorno uses the word autonomy, Osborne claims, as a speculative notion as opposed to a concrete goal. This is to say that the word is not formally defined, yet advocates striving for autonomy and creative expression as opposed to uniformity. The more the culture industry allows for diverse narratives and values, the more creative it is. This in turn allows for critical spectatorship.

Throughout his writings, it is evident that Adorno's thought evolves as reflected in his conversations and letters to Walter Benjamin and Siegfried Kracauer. In 'The Culture Industry Revisited' (1975), Adorno slightly modifies his initial claim that audiences are completely passive, asserting that audiences do mistrust authority which allows them to distinguish between art (or mass art) and reality. Several years later when interviewed on the radio, Adorno seemed surprized that the masses were able to, 'critically assess the political and social implications of the event' (Hansen, 1981–1982, p. 60), in this case, the wedding of Dutch Princess Beatrix to a German diplomat. He was forced to conclude that complete manipulation of the masses by those in power via the culture industry is not possible. Similarly, he acknowledged that the consciousness of the masses is (or could be) varied, multiple and dynamic.

This theoretical progress Adorno makes reflects the changes in mass art at the time he is writing, from the monopoly of the Hollywood Studio system in the 1930s and 1940s to the increased diversification in the industry. From my perspective, this progress also increases the plausibility of Adorno's ethical, political and economic concerns with regard to mass art. Although Adorno's conclusions are overstated and draw from a specific cultural context, his ethical concerns should not be so quickly dismissed. While it may not be the case that monopolising capitalist and consumerist forces will eventually ensure that we homogenize until we are devoid of individuality and distinction, the threat of being encouraged to passively ingest 'facts' from a variety of technological sources without critical reflection is a worrying prospect.

This prospect is grounds for acknowledging Adorno's later essay 'Transparencies on Film' as encouraging a subtle re-think of cinema as produced and displayed in an ideological context.

In this laters, Adorno claims:

> In its attempt to manipulate the masses the ideology of the culture industry itself becomes as internally antagonistic as the very society which it aims to control. The ideology of the culture industry contains the antidote to its own life. No other plea could be made for its defence. (p. 202)

Films allow for diverse voices to be heard and screened, Adorno now acknowledges in 'Transparencies on Film' (1981–1982). In this way, the culture industry gives expression to repressed or minority values which could possibly rise up against the dominant ideology, if not given an outlet. Yet, even if various voices are depicted, it is the dominant values that are ultimately reinforced. For example, 'while intention is always directed against the playboy, the dolce vita and wild parties, the opportunity to behold them seems to be relished more than the hasty verdict (pp. 201–202).' In depicting these images, Adorno claims, the culture industry reinforces them. Adorno notes the complexity of the relationship between film and society. If technology and cinema go hand in hand, so too do accompanying social values. Adorno claims, 'There could be no aesthetics of the cinema, not even a purely technological one, which would not include the sociology of the cinema (p. 202).' In this way, cinema cannot be purely aesthetic; it must also link to society and with social concerns.

Continuing the Conversation with Walter Benjamin

When critiquing social, political and economic factors that influence the production and uptake of mass artworks, it is useful to read Adorno alongside Benjamin. Benjamin offers an optimistic account of the (politically, socially and personally) emancipatory potential of art as it develops technologically, even though he also recognizes that commodities may be fetishized when used for their economic value and political and social power. Osborne details Benjamin's attitude to mass art:

> Because modern experience just *is* technological it is right that art itself should be expressive of this. Art can serve as a means of mastering the elemental forces of a technological second nature. Photography and film accustom humanity to the new apperceptions conditioned by technology. Technological art—like film and photography—becomes the site of exploration of future relations between technology and the human. (p. 60)

Certainly this has been proven as technology continues to advance and our use of it builds upon existing modes of self-expression. Benjamin and Adorno agreed that, in comparison to Art proper, the technological reproduction of mass art strips the artwork of its 'aura' or unique artistic quality. Adorno argues that loss of the aura of a work of art results in the simultaneous erosion of the artwork's aesthetic value. Yet, this is not the case for Benjamin. As Osborne articulates, for Benjamin, 'contrary to Adorno, the end of the aura is not necessarily negative in its consequences' (p. 61).

However, Benjamin is not offering a directly oppositional thesis to Adorno. Benjamin acknowledges that there are many social effects in response to mass art, one being that, 'the film responds to the shriveling of the aura with an artificial build-up of the "personality" outside the studio' (1969, p. 224). Adorno and Benjamin both see the technologically reproducible artwork as historical and contextual. In this way, mass art will continue to evolve.

By reading Adorno alongside Benjamin and by acknowledging the power of films to be potentially constructive (allowing for autonomy) or destructive (fetishizing the product for ideological or economic means), we get a more holistic vision of cinema as a socially situated activity. There is a need to focus on the critical attitude of the viewer, as well as the moral messages of the medium. This is particularly apparent when we consider what is watched by the majority of consumers. Adorno and Benjamin both offer a historical account of art whereby their aesthetics require audience reception and are linked to experience. Film communicates ideas and values that are received by viewers. While there are many different stories being told in contemporary culture, the focus on the critical thinker, the interpreter of the narrative, is vital in order to form a thinking society.

Adorno's method sometimes appears paradoxical and his principle of negative dialectics suggests we know freedom through its negation and, likewise, autonomy when we are restricted. It is through the paradox of knowing what is not an example of freedom or autonomy that allows us to aim at what is and, Osborne points out, these terms are not defined in a positive or epistemic manner. Rather, the terms operate as paradoxes in order for us to work towards liberty and autonomy. Osborne writes, 'One cannot simply posit freedom as if it could be unproblematically known: one is better occupied on a more negative task, in diagnosing the forces of unfreedom' (p. 39).

While Adorno worries about Hollywood Studio films, Benjamin focuses more of the avant-garde, the films of Eisenstein. Benjamin's optimism may be partly a result of the artworks with which he engages. Osborne claims,

> Benjamin is diagnosing the progressive or at least redemptive potentiality of modern forms of mass art. Adorno's whole question seems to be quite different from this: to measure the modern culture industry in ultimately ethical terms, that is, in terms of its relation to the forces of critical self-reflection. Where Adorno sees regression, Benjamin sees possibility; but this is a difference that is the product of their differing critical styles more than anything else. (p. 62)

Osborne's comparison reveals that Benjamin and Adorno are not using the same methodology, nor are they offering oppositional arguments. Thus, they both offer useful ideas to contemporary theorists of film and philosophy. Indeed, Adorno's critique of Benjamin is useful in offering a subtle re-reading of both. Adorno laments Benjamin's lack of a dialectical perspective (p. 62). Adorno writes to Benjamin on 18 March 1936:

> In your earlier writings … you distinguished the idea of the work of art as a structure from the symbol of theology on the one hand, and from the taboo of magic on the other. I now find it somewhat disturbing—and here I can see a sublimated remnant of certain Brechtian themes—that you have now rather casually transferred the concept of the magical aura to the 'autonomous work of work' and flatly assigned a counter-revolutionary function to the latter. (p. 128)

The question of whether the mass artwork is valuable as a tool to prompt critical thinking becomes tied to the idea that it does, or does not, have an aura. As seen in Adorno's quote above, the definition of what an aura is changes and is unclear. Benjamin defines 'aura' as 'A strange weave of space and time: the unique appearance or semblance of distance, no matter how close it may be' (Benjamin, 1991, pp. 518–519). Deleuze echoes this definition in the concepts of time and space on which he focuses his Cinema books written in the 1980s. Fredric Jameson calls attention to the dialectic occurring between Benjamin and Adorno, explaining,

> Riposting against Benjamin's attack on aesthetic 'aura' as a vestige of bourgeois culture and his celebration of the progressive function of technological reproducibility in art as the pathway to a new appropriation of it by the masses - realized above all in the cinema, Adorno replied with a defence of avant-garde art and a counter-attack against over-confidence in commercial-popular art. (Bloch Lukacs, Brecht, Benjamin, & Adorno, 1977, p. 106)

For Adorno, the beauty of the work of art *qua* artwork is that it does not tie up its ideas neatly and instead challenges the receiver to view reality in its representation, replete with its tensions and discordance. If art allows the viewer to see that there are multiple perspectives, it encourages critical spectatorship. In this way, 'art is negative knowledge of the actual world' (1967, p. 32). Adorno here refers to the method of negative dialectics whereby one recognizes the paradoxes in society and can thus be a critical or active thinker. If mass art can allow for the same understanding, it fails to be limited to a homogenous status quo.

Jameson suggests that contemporary philosophers of film have much to gain from revisiting the conversation that occurred between Adorno and Benjamin. He concludes:

> The force of many of these arguments remains pertinent today. It is clear that Benjamin, following Brecht, tended to hypostasize techniques in abstraction from relations of production, and to idealize diversions in ignorance of the social determinants of their production. His theory of the positive significance of distraction were based on a specious generalization from architecture, whose forms are always directly used as practical objects and hence necessarily command a distinct type of attention from those of drama, cinema, poetry or painting. …Where Benjamin manifestly overestimated the progressive destiny of the commercial-popular of his time, Adorno no less clearly over-estimated that of the avant-garde art of the period. (Bloch et al., 1977, pp. 107–108)

The letters between Benjamin and Adorno between 1935 and 1939 reveal much of the strengths and weaknesses of both writers' theories. The publication of these letters in English in 1999 invoked resurgence in interest in both scholars, particularly Adorno, who has been somewhat neglected by philosophy of film scholars' attraction to the more optimistic writings of Benjamin. Adorno insightfully recognizes the 'psychogistic subjectivism and ahistorical romanticism' in Benjamin's work and notes the Spinozean influence upon Benjamin that could develop in one of two extreme directions: it can be taken as a primal nostalgia for unity with nature: an unbridled romanticism; or as a utopian vision of classlessness that lacks class (or 'taste') entirely (Bloch et al., 1977, p. 103). The problem being that both perspectives are ungrounded, floating in a de-contextualized space, not linked to social reality, time and place. In this way, both perspectives become overly subjective and emotive. This critical insight Adorno has into Benjamin's work is one reason we should reconsider his critique of, not only Benjamin's optimism but of the contemporary approach towards philosophy and film as a technologically mass-produced and consumed medium (Bloch et al., 1977, p. 104). This is not to argue that we should adopt Adorno's negative critique wholesale either, but, as we wish to promote critical engagement in viewers of films, so too may philosophers critically engage with both Adorno and Benjamin.

Conclusion

As Bernstein has written, 'Adorno's is not so much an 'objective' analysis as a perspectival one' (cited in Osborne, 2008, p. 63). The perspectives offered by Adorno and Benjamin may give us cause to reconsider film and philosophy, particularly with reference to film spectatorship. Mass art is democratic in its accessibility and it is because of this social nature of film that we should celebrate what may be expressed through film and also be mindful of potential impact upon viewers.

Films may promote a critical response to society; yet, it may be that such films are already preaching to the converted. Teaching audiences to think critically is vital, particularly when other technological mediums are considered such as broadcast news, the internet, blogs and other social networking sites. Furthermore, there are practical implications and ethical concerns that mass untutored audiences, including children, are watching films that may contain unethical messages. In light of this, the focus on the critical viewer, with the educative notion of teaching viewers to be critical, is worth further consideration.

The concept of the value of the artwork, how it should be valued (aesthetically and ethically), its affect (its impact upon viewers, its critical reception as well as its production, including the intention of the author(s)) are all important issues. Where there is the potential for positive or life-affirming messages or affect being conveyed, there is equally the potential for the transmission of life-denying or nihilistic messages. If mass art encourages viewers to critique society, Adorno and Benjamin would claim that this is a good thing. However, where passive viewing is promoted, we must ask what values are being uncritically ingested and whether or not this has an effect on viewers and on society. Ultimately, I will conclude that we do not need censorship;

rather, we need critical reception and a continued conversation. This is of utmost importance in a world where so much is uncritically ingested and mass messages are transmitted and seductively screened ubiquitously. To paraphrase Adorno, the art will only change when its audiences do. There is still a need for philosophy proper and philosophical thinking skills and they should continue to be applied to film.

Note

1. *Fast & Furious 5* is listed by Screen Australia as one of the Top 50 films in Australia ranked by reported gross earnings. Director Justin Lin is up to #6 (2013) with #7 due for release in 2014.

References

Adorno, T. W. (1967). *Prisms*. (Samuel and Shierry Weber, Trans.). Cambridge: MIT Press.

Adorno, T. W. (1975). Culture industry reconsidered. *New German Critique, 6*, 12–19.

Adorno, T. W. (1981–1982). Transparencies on film. (T. Y. Levin, Trans.). *New German Critique*, Special Double Issue on New German Cinema, 24/25, 199–205.

Adorno, T. W., & Benjamin, W. (1999). *The complete correspondence 1928–1940*. (H. Lonitz, Ed., N. Walker, Trans.). Cambridge: Harvard University Press.

Adorno, T. W., & Horkheimer, M. (1997). The culture industry: Enlightenment as mass deception. In Adorno & Horkheimer (Eds.), *Dialectic of enlightenment*. London: Verso.

Benjamin, W. (1969). The work of art in the age of mechanical reproduction. (H. Zorn, Trans.). In H. Arendt (Ed.), *Illuminations* (pp. 217–252). New York, NY: Schocken Books.

Benjamin, W. (1991). *Selected writings*. (H. Eiland & M. W. Jennings, Eds.). Cambridge: Harvard University Press.

Bloch, E., Lukacs, G., Brecht, B., Benjamin, B., & Adorno, T. (1977). *Aesthetics and Politics*. (R Taylor, Trans.). Radical Thinkers Series. London: Verso.

Brummett, B. (2013). What popular films teach us about values: Locked inside with the rage virus. *Journal of Popular Film and Television, 41*, 61–67.

Carroll, N. (1998). *A philosophy of mass art*. Oxford: Clarendon Press.

Carroll, N. (2004). The power of movies. In P. Lamarque & S. H. Olsen (Eds.), *Aesthetics and the philosophy of art: The analytic tradition* (pp. 485–497). Oxford: Blackwell.

Collingwood, R. G. (1969). *The principles of art*. Oxford: Oxford University Press.

Colman, F. (2011). *Deleuze & cinema: The film concepts*. Oxford: Berg.

Deleuze, G. (1986). *Cinema I: The movement-image*. (H. Tomlinson & B. Habberjam, Trans.). Minneapolis, MN: University of Minnesota Press.

Deleuze, G. (1989). *Cinema II: The time-image*. Minneapolis, MN: University of Minnesota Press.

Hansen, M. (1981–1982). Introduction to Adorno, 'transparencies on film' (1966). *New German Critique, Special Double Issue on New German Cinema*, 24/25, 186–198.

Levine, M. (2001a). *Depraved spectators & impossible audiences: Horror and other pleasures of the cinema* (pp. 63–71). Special Edition on Horror: Film and Philosophy.

Levine, M. (2001b). A fun night out: Horror and other pleasures of the cinema. *Senses of Cinema, 17*. http://www.sensesofcinema.com

Markus, G. (2001). Walter Benjamin or: The commodity as phantasmagoria. *New German Critique, 83*, 3–42.

McCann, P. (2008). *Race, music, and national identity: Images of jazz in American fiction, 1920–1960*. Delaware: Associated University Press.

Osborne, T. (2008). *The structure of modern cultural theory*. Manchester, NH: Manchester University Press.

Osborne, P., & Charles, M. (2011). Walter Benjamin. In E. N. Zalta (Ed.), *The Stanford encyclopedia of philosophy*. http://plato.stanford.edu/archives/spr2011/entries/benjamin/
Wartenberg, T. E. (2006). Beyond mere illustration: How films can be philosophy. *The Journal of Aesthetics and Art Criticism, 64*, 19–32.
Wartenberg, T. E. (2007). *Thinking on screen: Film as philosophy*. London: Routledge.

Film Bibliography

Armageddon. (1998). Dir. Michael Bay.
Fast & Furious 5. (2012). Dir. Justin Lin.
Melancholia. (2011). Dir. Lars von Trier.
Modern Times. (1936). Dir. Charles Chaplin.
The Matrix. (1999). Dir. The Wachowskis.

Reconsidering Music's Relational Dimension: Heidegger and the work of music in education

DAVID LINES

Abstract

This essay considers the way and manner in which a musician and music educator approaches his or her work. It is suggested that anthropomorphic conceptions of music have endured in music education practice in the West. It is proposed that our view of the 'processes' of music making, music reception and music learning can be challenged and reconsidered. Heidegger's theory of art is used as a way of rethinking these processes, and of reconsidering our relational dimension with music. The unfolding of music in music-events occurs as people 'work-with' music and interact with its dimensions in a way that is culturally and dialogically vibrant. Music education can thus become more responsive to changing 'modes of beings' in the moment.

Musicians hold various perspectives about the nature of their work. For some, the music making process is deeply personal and creative: they consider that their work is dedicated to the original creation of special works and performances. Other musicians are more attuned to the professional nature of their work: they perform their music with specific regard to the functional purpose to which their music making is orientated, making sure standards are upheld in the process. Some put importance on understanding the 'scientific' components of great music works through methods of analysis, aesthetic appreciation, and other forms of study. Others become focused on the prowess of their own skill and craft and their capacity to unleash musical sounds with a degree of technical competency that they judge to be adequate. These perspectives focus on the level of ability, competence and analytical understandings of the musicians themselves, on the proficiency of human music makers. To what extent, however, do these perspectives dominate philosophical positions of music education and music education practice? My argument, here, is that music education in the West has appropriated a particular disabling view of what it means to be a player, singer, composer or listener of music in today's society: the human acts as a sovereign autonomous creator, performer or receiver of music in a functional environment of musical 'contract' or 'need'. These views of music activity can be questioned. In addition to the actions of the individual performer/composer/receiver of music we can think about the historicity, influence and intensity of 'cultural work' (Lines, 2003) at play.

Heidegger's writing about art leads me to consider an alternative view of art making, one that does not put the intent and work of the sovereign artist in the forefront of artistic action—as an ends-driven exercise. In this essay I argue that rather than considering music/art to be work geared towards ourselves, by ourselves, we can, as Heidegger suggests, think about this kind of work as 'working with' music/art. I propose that if music educators adopt this kind of ethical disposition—one that 'works with' and 'cares for' the artistic process—they have the potential to guide students into a way of learning that is more musical and resonant with the cultural communities in which they reside.

The position of the individual human musical subject as 'sovereign, autonomous creator' has an equal bearing on the status of the musical object. When one considers the human musical subject in a detached, autonomous sense, the 'object' of sovereign creation—music—becomes constituted as an autonomous work of art. Such a view treats music as a singular entity, divorced or set apart from other things in the world that may establish some kind of configuration with it. Similarly, musical systems become 'disciplined', in a Foucaudian sense[1]: processes of production, dissemination, reception and education in music serve to perpetuate and repeat instances of musical objectification, in obedient response to the discursive power relations of a time and place. The processes of objectification have a neutralising effect; they nullify the penetrating properties of music and restrict its resonance with communities of cultural work that constitute its emergence. In such circumstances music becomes a debilitating force with no particular educational or artistic resonance in everyday life. I maintain that in Western industrialised countries, music has been somewhat reduced to that of an *object-being*, an entity that 'shows up' as an object of the subjectivity of the mind's powers. The anthropocentrism of Enlightenment thinking pervades our conceptualisation and reception of music and becomes further accentuated when music events succumb to forces of commodification and exchange. The place of musical engagement requires some theoretical investigation and this, in turn, has a bearing on the place, nature and value of music education. Rather than focusing on the necessary skills of the musician or his or her theoretical object—music—in the first instance, I argue here that a music pedagogy can be constituted from an ethical and artistic engagement with what comes forth in a musical event.

A Heideggerian Perspective of Music

My particular position on music and music education, elaborated here, is drawn from the later (post *Being and Time*) philosophy of Martin Heidegger. While Heidegger does not engage directly in discussion on music, his theoretical position on art provides some insight into the nature of the musical experience. In his seminal essay *The Origin in the Work of Art*, Heidegger gives considerable thought to the topic at hand: the critique of the conscious subject and the objectification of the art-object. These themes however need to be seen in relation to Heidegger's larger project of being and it is to this broader context that I turn first.

What is Heidegger's Being and beings? Heidegger's thinking of Being and beings is focussed on the necessity to view things as they are, as beings in their existence that appear momentarily as truth (*aletheia*) amidst a conglomeration and contestation of different beings manifest as different shades of revealing. For Heidegger, the questioning of Being is pivotal, for it has been forgotten. He reminds us, that due to their temporal nature, we never quite know what beings really are. Beings are not fixed absolutes but, rather, illusive, fluid and temporal configurations of the moment. Beings can be things, works of art, music, thoughts, emotions, values and humans, in fact, anything that shows up as something, which 'is' (Dreyfus, 2002). The showing up of beings—'world'—is only possible because of an ontological horizon that Heidegger broadly calls 'earth'. Heidegger's idea of 'earth' is similar to his idea of Being. The broader definition of Being (noted with a capital B) is 'the quiet power of the possible' (Heidegger, 1993b, p. 221). Being (capitalised) is the 'ground, "sufficient reason" or "ultimate possibility" of the articulated structure of beings ... as that which first makes beings possible' (Bartky, 1970, p. 370).

Different beings have different modes that interrelate during instances of affect and power. Within the space opened up as a world, the area of contestation is fluid and lively. One being may place itself in front of another being (obscure it), or alternatively, one may deny the revealing of another. This amounts to an understanding of plural beings working with and against each other (Heidegger, 1993a, p. 179). All beings are revealed in events, each fresh instance coming forth as a cycle of change. Similarly, music draws together particular synchronic configurations of beings in events and unfolds as its territories are revealed moment by moment. Musics, then, in this Heideggerian sense, are diverse 'modes of beings', that when revealed, enter an artistic world of change and differentiation.

How, then, can we come to understand a musician's work in a way that is real and engaging, in a way that also acknowledges and works with Being and beings? It would be correct to say that this question is of prime importance for the music educator, as pedagogue, who is involved in the cultural regeneration and transformation of musical *life* from one generation to another. The music educator works with processes of musical transmission and change, processes that require attunement to the fluid forces at work in a cultural epoch and historical community. Working with changes, shades and different qualities of beings requires a certain active disposition, an understanding and repositioning of things as they stand in relation to the human condition. This amounts to a re-perception of the immediate control of human work and upon this position, the *projecting, caring, and preserving* of beings—'*working with*' them into new points of unconcealedness. Such a music educator is attuned to the changing way that the dimensions music experiences are revealed and concealed. By attending to a critical understanding of music as a culturally embedded art form, Bowie (1999) notes, we can look for the ways in which we come to view and apprehend music—as it shows up. This field of engagement is appropriate, for it allows us to work with, examine and care for a 'continuing interaction of different historical horizons' (p. 6) in music. What makes art 'true', or 'revealed to us', is not confined to a human centred conception of art, or one historical perspective. Music, as it comes forth, is created, produced and received in relation to an historical horizon of plural 'truths'. For the music educator, an ability to navigate this region of plurality would seem to be fundamentally important.

Heidegger places questions of art and thinking within the horizon of time. For him, the objectification of what is 'present-at-hand'—the way modern science observes and calculates things as objects for human use—is a condition of metaphysical thinking that conceals a horizon of temporality. Nothing can escape the rubric of time, not the least, the fluid and changing art of music. There is a synergy between beings and temporality and by reinforcing this synergy Heidegger questions the widespread tendency to objectify art—a tendency that contributes to the 'impotence' of the art and art education worlds. For Heidegger, questions of art and thinking should turn to questions of process, movement and change; the way that things appear as events and are worked by artists. In this sense thinking is best considered as what comes forth and actioned in the momentary performative act—speaking. 'Only when man speaks, does he think—not the other way around, as metaphysics still believes' (Heidegger, 1993d, p. 381). Art, too, in this view, is revealed in the momentary expressions of events as artistic actions synchronise with the historical and communal forces, meanings and practices from which they emerge.

The pedagogical implications of these points indicate that the music educator requires more than an impression of musical modes of being in the present. A critical educator who works with changing musical modes will question the ground on which musical beings (in a plural sense) show up in an 'Event' (*Ereignis*) and how this is viewed in relation to changing historical beings. If temporality is germane to Being, we can ask the question: How have beings changed? How have things shown themselves? Dreyfus (2002) writes of the dominant ways beings have shown up and remained (endured) in different historical epochs, as analysed by Heidegger; and also, comparatively with French philosopher Michel Foucault. Dreyfus notes that in Heidegger's view, things have shown up 'for the Greeks as *physis* (self disclosing), for the Romans as finished pieces of work, for the Medievals as creatures, for the early modern age as objects, and for us moderns as resources to be ordered for efficient further enhancement' (Dreyfus, 1992, p. 3). Heidegger's observations of how things have shown up also have similarities with Foucault's genealogical analyses of the 'self': the Greek caring of the self, the Stoics management of the self-imposing form, the medieval understanding of the self as created being (Dreyfus, 2002). Dreyfus' outlines of these thinkers' ideas are helpful for they begin to clear the ground of forgotten being in history.

More recently, in what has been referred to as the 'modern age', or modernity—post seventeenth century European culture and thought—the history of beings has taken on a more decidedly anthropomorphic character of change. The origins of these changes can be traced back to Platonic and Roman humanistic beliefs. The change has been an increasing division between human subjective sensing/thinking and the outwardness or objectification of the 'other', thing, artwork or technological implement. Descartes' separation of mind and body and his implicit introduction of representation (where material things are represented in the human mind) became explicit in Kant's notion of 'Vorstellung' (the knowing and imaging of objects in our senses) (Dreyfus, 2002). Similarly Hegel's idealism or transcendental 'absolute spirit' where the realm of creative idea is situated in a theological context, indirectly (i.e. the human context becomes a vehicle for the work of God) indicates a pattern of thought where beings show up as objects in the *human* gaze.

Gadamer (1994), who interprets Heidegger in a number of essays published in *Heidegger's Ways*, comments on the way aesthetics developed from the time of the founder of the autonomous aesthetic concept—Alexander Baumgarten. He notes that only within the explicit restriction of Enlightenment rationalism in the eighteenth century was the 'autonomous right of sensuous knowledge asserted and with it the relative independence of the judgement of taste from the understanding and its concepts' (p. 100). He also notes that basing aesthetics on the subjectivity of the mind, as developed by Kant and the neo-Kantian thinkers, was a 'dangerous process of subjectification' (p. 101); initially presupposing a 'theological idea of creation'; then with the decline in the power of religious forces, assuming an ontological model that assumed the 'systematic priority of scientific cognition' (p. 102). Gadamer uses the word 'dangerous' to imply the inhibiting and reductive effect of the aesthetic paradigm on artistic (musical) culture. Aesthetic perception and contemplation, points not only to the value of the transcendent idea or form, but also to the centrality of the sovereign subject in relation to what is an appearance or 'other'. To Heidegger, this progression of thinking and its manifestation, is what he calls 'metaphysics', the characteristic of historical thinking that has forgotten being. Through aesthetics the creation of art is viewed in a particular way of thinking that reveres the subject. 'Modern subjectivism, to be sure, immediately misinterprets creation, taking it as the sovereign subject's performance of genius' (Heidegger, 1993a, p. 200).

It was in the context of these developments in aesthetic thinking that Heidegger presented the *Origin of the Work of Art* lecture in 1936. The lecture created a philosophical sensation as it directly questioned the assumptions about the nature of the work of art as explored in the field of aesthetics (Gadamer, 1994). As Gadamer (one of Heidegger's students) noted, scripts of this lecture were widely disseminated and became the subject of intense discussion. It was Heidegger's original counter-concepts of 'world' and 'earth', Gadamer reports, that were of most interest to the speculative philosophical public. Although 'world' was the familiar horizon of disclosure presented in Heidegger's seminal *Being and Time*, the new concept 'earth' represented a fundamentally new way of conceiving art—the 'necessary determination of the Being of the work of art' (p. 100). This firmly acknowledged the field of Being as distinct from the region of absolute human intention. The introduction Heidegger's thought of 'earth' into serious thinking about art, challenged prevailing aesthetic thinking dominated by Enlightenment notions of the subjectivity of the mind's powers.

In the *Origin of the Work of Art* Heidegger thinks the distinction of matter and form is the 'conceptual schema that is used, in the greatest variety of ways, quite generally for all art theory and aesthetics' (Heidegger, 1993a, p. 153). In Heidegger's perspective, it is aesthetic formalism that has endured in modernity (i.e. since the

Enlightenment), manifesting itself as an objectified preconception of the artwork. He sees the aesthetic way of thinking as a conceptual machinery (an enframing[2] of the aesthetic thought-world) that nothing is capable of withstanding (Heidegger, 1993a, p. 153). It has led to belief in 'matter-form' as a specification leading to the nature of the artwork. A technical, or, as Heidegger suggests, 'equipmental' view of art, is more akin to the technological production of equipment than the creative art process. The equipmental conception of the artwork is primarily seen in terms of the resource matter of the material used and the equipmental structure of its form. In contemporary society, Heidegger argues, the matter-form distinction now constitutes the primary understanding of beings, not only in art, but in all elements of culture.

> The matter-form structure, however, by which the Being of a piece of equipment is first determined, readily presents itself as the immediately intelligible constitution of *every* being, because here man himself as maker participates in the way in which the piece of equipment comes into being. Because equipment takes an intermediate place between mere thing and work, the suggestion is that non-equipmental beings—things and works and ultimately all beings—are to be comprehended with the help of the Being of equipment (the matter-form structure) (Heidegger, 1993a, p. 155, my italics).

Heidegger is referring here to something more widespread than mere cultural artefacts. He extends his observation of the dominance of pre-figured form to all beings. Thus, in the present epoch, Heidegger maintains that we tend to perceive of our own being and other beings in the sense of pre-figured form rather than what beings actually 'are'. This notion of an overriding configuration of dominating thought is elaborated further in Heidegger's essay *A Question Concerning Technology* (Heidegger, 1993c, pp. 311–341) where he presents his concept of Gestell (enframing). The configuration of Gestell is such that people cannot see outside its perspective. It 'enframes' the way people think about beings in the moment including music's modes of beings.

Heidegger's Gestell-aesthetic does appear to be predominant in today's global culture. Gestell configures the global thought patterns, images and sounds of commodification and corporate business. Examples include the repetitive multimedia designs of corporate branding (a mere stroll through various shopping malls in Western countries confirms this). In music, the commodified, stylistic fetishisms of popular culture influence configurations of identity, labelling, fashion and attitude. Gestell can be observed in the manufactured TV pop bands whose appealing music are a subtle mix of effective musical 'hooks', stylistic blends of well-worn pop arrangements, and youthful, sexy, video images. Similarly, the classical music world submits to perfectionist score details and digital concert sound in the reproduction of the great iconic classical works. Collectively, these sonic cultural configurations form a 'world picture' of the Gestell relation in music that commodifies and objectifies music as a packaged entity.

A piece of music is commonly referred to as a 'music work'. This usage of the notion of work has become objectified: the musical work is a 'composed' piece, stored or recorded in either written score or digitised form, and reproduced or played, subsequently, in further repetitions of the same. Here, music's cultural work is physically encapsulated as visual scores or recorded digital CDs. These packaged conceptions of music practice are further influenced, no doubt, by the continuous expansion of the economically driven global CD culture. The Western consumer's 'music of perfection' remains a cultural force of some power and significance in the commodity driven contemporary, classical and world music fields (Keil & Feld, 1994).

The forces of the commercial art world pre-figure the work-beings of art works as commercial objects. Industrial power and the demands of commercial interests transform the workly character of art works to the degree that they can become permanently changed. Music, too, submits to forces of commercial interest. Our altered conceptions of well worn pop songs and famous classical pieces (the latter churned over endlessly in various permutations in the television and film industries) are testament to the extensive impact that forces of commodification and global media industries have on our reception of music—and ultimately music creation in the twenty first century.

In 1919, Heidegger wrote:

> The unbridled, basically Enlightenment directive to nail life and everything living onto a board, like things, orderly and flat, so that everything becomes oversee-able, controllable, definable, connectable and explicable, where only many pure and unrestrained 'ables' exist—this directive underlies all the quasi-memories of life, which are being attempted today in every sphere of experience. (Heidegger, 1919, cited in Thiele, 1995, p. 193)

This strongly measured quote (pre *Being and Time*) exemplifies the seriousness of Heidegger's thinking about the controlling, manipulating and technological character of modern culture, a passage all the more resonant in the present age given it was written over eighty years ago. The desire and need to control was seen by him as a specifically human problem, the genealogy of which could be observed in the spectre of humanism. The anthropomorphic human posits humankind at the centre of a universe made available for exploration and exploitation. Within the modern perspective of humanism, beings exist as resources—as objects for the human species—and they gather their value accordingly.

Where, then, is music situated in the humanistic drive for control? The intrusion of music as *object-being* is part of this controlling drive. It nullifies the capacity for music to act as an agent of educational change. Instead, the notion of *object-being* takes music to be an entity or equipmental object that exists for human consumption. An identifying feature of this condition is the lack of thought about Being (artistic capacity) itself, outside the objectification of the frame. Similarly, the Being of music is enframed in this way; in a manner that one cannot see it for what it is, in all its capacities and connections as the life-world. Enframing captures the work of music in this way through pedagogy. Music pedagogy encompasses both the enculturation of music and the overt intervention of music in the manner of institutional and commercial music education. The cultural objectification of music endures through the ways, practices and manifestations of music teaching and learning.

The enframing of music education is evident in the way we view the development of musically educated subjects and how we pedagogically gear ourselves to that orientation. To the enframed music educator, to be 'musical' means to accustom oneself and music students to the objectified production of music 'works' in the interests of commercial consumption or 'authentic' reproductions of iconic, sublime creations. Such an orientation treats the musician as a technically proficient subject or receptive analyst in the first instance, with little regard to cultural meaning, resonance and connection. This creates problems. Deprived of a sense of community meaning or resonance with the broader cultural work of music, music education institutions 'retreat' into their own efforts to legitimise themselves. These retentive actions do nothing for the enhancement of a living and breathing musically educated society. How, then, can music education become more resonant and significant in education and society at large? Is there an alternative conception of the human relation to music that music educators can embrace? In response to these questions we can consider Heidegger's provocative, revisionary, rethinking of art. Heidegger (1993a, p. 143) thinks we should return to an understanding of the relatedness of the facets that work together in the art experience.

'Working With' Music

Music making is a part of what all humans do in everyday activities: people 'produce' music. Producing or 'placing there' (Heidegger, 2001, p. 107) can be singing, listening, making, drawing, designing, thinking, speaking, arranging or expressing, in fact anything that involves an act of venture. It could be said, then, that producing is a human act through and through, part of our being or Being in a 'broad and multifarious sense' (Young, 2002, p. 47). 'Producing' is akin to 'working', in fact, working is a more appropriate term for what humans do, as it carries the notion of working-with others rather than the mere actions of an individual. The human could be said then to be a 'worker', someone who works with things in the world. Human work, in this sense, occurs within a wider region of power relations that 'play' with what is humanly projected.

In *The Origin of the Work of Art*, Heidegger initially draws the reader into an understanding of both equipmental and artistic senses of 'things'. The introductory part of this essay establishes the notion that Being is not the sole providence of human being but is applied to all 'things' in their existence. Being is thus plural and exudes the notion of difference. In *Identity and Difference* Heidegger (1960, p. 21) states: 'Obviously Man (sic) represents some Existent. As such, he belongs with the stone, the tree, and the eagle to the totality of Being. To belong is in this context still equivalent to being incorporated into Being', and in his *Letter on Humanism* he writes: 'Man (sic) does not decide whether and how beings appear, whether and how God or the gods or history and nature come forward into the clearing of Being, come to presence and depart' (Heidegger, 1993b, p. 234). Art works 'shine' in a world opened up by them in their own being in a way that is apart from human intervention. By recognising the 'outside' character of art-works Heidegger simultaneously disassembles any humanistic conceptions of art that might be lingering in the reader. An affirmation of the 'shining' of art draws attention to the world that is opened up when art is 'set-up', a world that is in many ways independent from the gaze of the author or creator. This view of art work is different from the formalist conception of art (as in traditional aesthetics) that carries with it a metaphysical assumption: beauty of form is a reflection of the exquisite structure of the work and/or the creative genius of the artist. Rather, Heidegger asks: what is the workly character of the work? What does the work do apart from the creator of it? As beings, art works project truths within the historical context of a people. These truths exist in the region of cultural emergence and change rather than as fixed notions of beautiful form or the mystic ideas of the creative genius. The artist diminishes as the work emerges.

Heidegger recognises that an autonomous view of 'things' is not sufficient for it negates the influence and interaction of the artist, who after all, is the creator of a work. Once the thought of the 'shining' work (apart from human intervention) as *poiësis* (emergent creating) is established, he then proceeds to outline out of that, what the consequential role of the human is, in relation to the work. By doing this, Heidegger's style is less 'violent' or intrusive than more common human-centred approaches to art for an ethic of respect and care of being is established. The resulting language tends to have a more 'theological' sound to it … a work is 'set up'—it is an establishing that lets us 'consecrate and praise'—the work demands it—because it opens a world and keeps it abidingly in force (Heidegger, 1993a, p. 169). Later in *The Origin of the Work of Art* essay he states: 'Preserving the work does not reduce people to their private experiences, but brings them into affiliation with the truth happening in the work' (p. 193). The human actions implied here have a caring quality about them and for this reason Heidegger's work has become attractive to the disciplines of ecology and conservation. Heidegger's human is a gentle and caring character who works with things with the intent of preservation—*'working with'* things and *'letting'* them be as they are.

Heidegger says that art is the origin of both the creators and preservers, and an existential element in our historical existence (p. 200). The pedagogical style of the artist-educator, then, is to have 'reverence' for the nature of art that is part of her being. Recognising art as an origin is a crucial element in such a pedagogy. The sovereign or instrumental-humanist subject does not recognise the profundity of this notion. The artist-educator however has a crucial role in the recovery of the origin of art and the transformation of an impotent artistic culture. The recovery involves acting with a certain disposition and respect for the artistic process. The artist 'projects' (Heidegger, 1993a, p. 198) her work by nominating it, naming it, bringing it forth in the same way that people have used language to name things and have projected them forward into historical awareness (Heidegger called language the 'house of being' (Heidgger, 1993b, p. 217)). The artist also 'sets' and 'fixes' in place the self-establishing truth of art works in the way of a 'figure'—that is, the specific configuration and set of mediating forces that establishes a work of art.

Conclusions and Implications for Music Education

This reading of Heidegger's philosophy of art has implications for the work of the music educator at many different levels. First, one might note the implications of the perspective of musics as 'modes of beings'. Musical modes of beings form configurations with musicians involved in their conception, development, performance, production, appreciation and dissemination. Theorising music as modes of beings means *working with* music in a number of layers including dimensions of creation (*poiësis*), ways of knowing (*technë*), action and planning (setting up), performance (setting forth), shining (truth, unconcealing) and reception (engagement in historical and communal contexts). Musical modes of beings involve both human interaction (preserving, caring, shaping, projecting) and letting music be what it is in its own existence.

In music, the emerging contestation of a work is played out in sound spaces. As music is played, its reception is granted according to the way that musical processes are activated and engaged, in relation to beings involved in and with the work. Further, each music work engages with the historical sound experiences of a community. Historical and communal forces come into play, forces that a musician and music educator can seek to understand and enter a dialogue with. The dialogue can be realised if the worker is able to work freely with the interacting forces that resonate in a music moment. How can one establish a free relation with the interactive spaces of music play? Such a disposition is nurtured through an appreciation of what makes music *poiësis* possible. The music educator working in such a perspective thus acknowledges, articulates and *cares for* the processes and configurations that enable music experiences to become what they are. He or she *sets up* and *lets* synchronicity happen in music.

In terms of education in music, Heidegger's thinking provides a rich framework for music *praxis*. The preparation of a musical performance, for instance, would take into account the subtle nuances a work may exude, as a work, along with the 'setting forth' and deciding of specific historical/contextual modes of awareness the work at hand demands. These decisions might influence aspects of performance including performance-space, pedagogical relevance, setting, musical interpretation, association with other forms of art/media, and metaphoric indicators. The self-reflective nature of these kinds of performance *praxes* would encourage critical questioning of the multi-dimensions of beings that emerge.

Finally, a music educator can prepare, 'set up' and 'work with' experiences of musical action that generate *musical* questioning, thinking and interpretation. Active, momentary dimensions of music emerge when musical modes of beings are unconcealed. Responding to these occurrences of unconcealment involves a degree of careful pedagogical planning and action. This requires learning and knowing about the dimensions and 'spaces' of music, and the critical dimensions of cultural/historical patterns that effect music learning and action. When these dimensions are given greater precedence, the question, 'what is musical?', has a transformed significance. It becomes a changing concept that *works with* music.

Notes

1. See *Discipline and Punish* (Foucault, 1977).
2. Enframing is Heidegger's name for the way modern technology encapsulates and 'enframes' predetermined ways of thinking in the modern epoch.

References

Bartky, S. (1970) Originative Thinking in the Later Philosophy of Heidegger, *Philosophy and Phenomenological Research*, 30:3, pp. 368–381.

Bowie, A. (1999) Adorno, Heidegger and the Meaning of Music, *Thesis Eleven*, 56, Feb 1999, pp. 1–23.

Dreyfus, H. (2002) *Being and Power: Heidegger and Foucault.* Cited on the www on 18/08/02 at http://ist-socrates.berkeley.edu/~hdreyfus/html/paper_being.html

Foucault, M. (1977) *Discipline and Punish*, trans. A. Sheridan (New York, Pantheon).

Gadamer, H. (1994) *Heidegger's Ways*, trans. J. Stanley, (Albany, State University of New York Press).

Heidegger, M. (1960) *Essays in Metaphysics: Identity and difference* (New York, Philosophical Library Inc).

Heidegger, M. (2001) *Poetry, Language, Thought*, trans. A. Hofstadter (New York, HarperCollins).

Heidegger, M. (1993a) The Origin of the Work of Art, in: D. Krell (ed.) *Basic Writings* (New York, HarperCollins).

Heidegger, M. (1993b) Letter on Humanism, in: D. Krell (ed.) *Basic Writings* (New York, HarperCollins).

Heidegger, M. (1993c) The Question Concerning Technology, in: D. Krell (ed.) *Basic Writings* (New York, HarperCollins).

Heidegger, M. (1993d) The Way to Language, in: D. Krell (ed.) *Basic Writings* (New York, HarperCollins).

Thiele, L. (1995) *Timely Meditations: Martin Heidegger and postmodern politics* (Princeton, Princeton University Press).

Keil, C. & Feld, S. (1994) *Music Grooves* (Chicago, University of Chicago Press).

Lines, D. (2003) *The Melody of the Event: Nietzsche, Heidegger and music education as cultural work* (Unpublished PhD Thesis, University of Auckland).

Young, J. (2002) *Heidegger's Later Philosophy* (Cambridge, Cambridge University Press).

Index

INDEX

www.ingramcontent.com/pod-product-compliance
Ingram Content Group UK Ltd.
Pitfield, Milton Keynes, MK11 3LW, UK
UKHW010021280225
455677UK00023B/723